WRITING SHORT STORIES FOR PLEA
PN
D0975143
A

WRITING SHORT STORIES
FOR
PLEASURE AND PROFIT

Marian Gavin

PUBLISHERS *The Writer, Inc.* BOSTON

Library of Congress Catalog Card Number: 73-3376
ISBN: 73-87116-081-1

Printed in the United States of America

PREFACE TO THE NEW EDITION

I wanted to mark this new edition of WRITING SHORT STORIES FOR PLEASURE AND PROFIT, which I wrote ten years ago, by telling you something completely new about storytelling. But I discovered that there are only a few primary truths that you can know about anything, and once you know them and tell them, that's it. You have no new primary thing to tell.

So I have now only new ways to tell the same old things about story that animated me ten years back, though I have learned more about them and know some of them better. And this is the other side of the coin— the marvelous side for storytellers: There is no end, *really no end,* to knowing and telling better and better what is real.

I know better now the value of stories: They are a lot more important to our lives than most of us commonly think. I also know that some stories are real, genuine in substance—while some are not. I believe we need stories to keep us human. But anyone sensible must concede that no genuine hunger and thirst are satisfied by the unreal, the counterfeit or the artificial, which serves nothing but its own "self," whether that "self" is delusion or illusion. Neither has substance.

Nothing, therefore, will do for our real need but real stories. And for that, there must be real storytellers. And who are they? They are the writers who know and practice storytelling as a *getting* and a *giving*—in that order. I call it "realizing the actual"—"actualizing the real."

Translated, "realizing the actual" means the getting of your story idea from your own unique experience of reality. "Actualizing the real" means fleshing out that unique experience of reality so that your reader can feel it, see it, *know it as his own.*

Storyteller, it's not so much what happens *to* you, as it is what happens *in* you, and what you make of that "happening," because *that* is all you have that is really your own to give: It is the spirit of your story, whatever new thing comes to life in you—your own expression of the reality you experience *in* you while or after the event happened *to* you.

All the rest is the geometry (structure) of your story, the calculations (inventions, techniques, special effects, practical enchantments) you must make to carry the spirit of your story to your reader's inner eye—that sight of heart and mind which should be your legitimate target.

The order is important: In storytelling, the spirit needs to come first; then the geometry is likely to follow, to come of itself to fit the spirit and make it visible. Begin with your own first-time experience of any of the common human events (birth, love, death), as they happen to each of us, moment by moment, within our own range of vision, outer and inner.

Language is your greatest help in getting the first thing you must have—the spirit of your story. Language is the only means you have to express what happens to you, in you. Without the idea, the spirit, no image will follow: Word and picture inseparable; meaning and form joined.

So, the new-knowings and the new-tellings of what one

finds to be real stretch on infinitely. Everything I have found—and still find—to be real in the creative art of storytelling is in this book, as I know it and told it ten years ago.

My hope is that the book will encourage and inspire you to get and give and rightly tell the real stories we all need.

—Marian Gavin

CONTENTS

WRITING SHORT STORIES
FOR
PLEASURE AND PROFIT

One

WRITING IS WHAT YOU MAKE IT

THE world takes many views of writers. Most laymen, bless their hearts, see a writer (if male) as a commanding figure in a velvet-collared smoking jacket, pipe in one hand, pen in the other, and the entire magnificent Presence housed in a book-lined study, all genuine leather and Persian carpet. If a woman, the writer is often pictured humming away in a sunny room, doing something remarkably similar to whipping up a batch of sugar cookies during a three-second lull between bedmaking and laundry.

Writers, on the other hand, see themselves and other writers (if they see other writers at all) as hunched, shadowy, sexless figures, each prisoned in his own dark, smoke-filled cell, creatures in unspeakable torment, forever exiled from life in any and all of its more pleasant manifestations.

Both of these viewpoints are ridiculous. Writing isn't and never will be just a large bowl of tutti-frutti for the person attempting it, but right now I'm going way out on a limb and state that if you write short stories in the too-often vain hope of selling them for *money,* this doesn't have to exclude you automatically from enjoying life—it can even insure that you *do* enjoy life. Is it absolutely necessary that Writing and Agony walk hand in hand? No, it isn't. Oh, certainly there's agony in writing. There is agony in most things worth doing. But, actually what *is* so agonizing about writing —aside from the fact that it's an impossibly difficult form of communication? I'll grant that. Writing is impossibly difficult. The difficulties are inherent, built in. The written word falls far short of the original basic forms of communication between human beings (also between bees and birds and ants, for all we know).

Here we are, substituting standardized marks on cool, dispassionate, soulless paper, which won't even be the same paper we wrote it on, won't even have our tears and sweat and the warmth of our hand on it by the time it reaches the hoped-for pinnacle of being published and read by people. This is a very frightening thing, to know that our competition is every physical person-to-person communication—auditory, visual, olfactory, sensory, from Adam's first remark to Eve and vice versa, every grunt, every glance, every whistle, every touch. And as if that weren't enough, the telephone had to be invented, radio, movies, and, finally, television—the big monster, the Trojan gift-horse which we allow in our homes and which devours, among other precious things, the time a family might spend in reading!

The difficulty of making the printed word mean anything to anybody is getting harder and harder all the time. And we have to go and make it even harder by limiting and hobbling, shutting ourselves up in a mean little box called a Short Story. But communication through the written word has always been hard. One glance between two people has always, admittedly, been worth—what is it?—a thousand words. Writers have always had to compete with lovers' glances and kisses, with hand clasps, with the spoken word, with music, vocal and instrumental, with visual art forms, with perfume and the taste of food, with sun and rain and thunder and lightning.

We have our nerve trying to communicate all this through the medium of little marks, usually black, on paper, usually white. But that's what we have and that's what it takes—nerve, and plenty of it. You may call it self-confidence, egomania, conceit, lack of modesty— but to me it's just plain old nerve.

You must have it! If you don't, beat your mental bushes until you find it. You won't get anywhere without it. If you're unable to find it, you may as well get off the writing track; writing is not for you.

We who remain face the fact that writing anything meaningfully is impossible—short stories in particular. But we have found nerve we didn't know we had, and now we are willing to tackle the impossible. We accept the challenge. Already we're beginning to dig in and enjoy this. Aren't we?

Along about this time we realize there are several slight advantages to writing as a means of communication. This is especially true of the short story. For one thing, it's short. Up to fifteen or sixteen pages of this precocious, impossible fabrication won't kill us, now will it?

At its very best, fiction, and especially short fiction, combines the impact of sight, sound, touch, smell and taste, memory and anticipation, plus moral and social values, which few of the other art and entertainment mediums can claim. The written word, even in a weekly or monthly magazine, is, I like to believe, somewhat less perishable than the number one rock 'n' roll hit-of-the-week. It is infinitely less perishable in the audience-participation sense than that thousand-word glance one man gives his wife on their anniversary; or the glance (which no one but God sees) of a murderer looking down at his victim; or a baby's first delighted seeing-glance up into his mother's face.

As story writers, we capture and affirm and re-affirm all these things for all people who can or care to read. Our potential range is as wide as human experience to date. This is true, I believe, even in the slick fiction story with all its apparent taboos. To me, a taboo results from a persistently unskillful, perverted, distasteful, disagreeable treatment of a subject by a great number of writers. I truly believe that anything can be written about, even for the slick magazines, if it is done with skill, compassion, taste and honesty. By honesty, I don't mean maudlin public confession or detailed self-pity or stark raving realism. That kind of realism is nothing but brutality, a form of sadism perpetrated on the reader by the author for reasons best known to himself.

There's a lot more satisfaction in being good to your readers, in being able to make free use of all the material at hand, not just a mean little fraction of it. We are limited in subject matter only by the wide boundaries enclosing all the matters, minute and vast, which touch the human spirit; we have a potential audience of millions, many as yet unborn. Notice that I did say potential! Whether we ever attain that potential or not, it is a very exciting thing to know that within our limits we are free; that we aren't so much competing with every other communication medium under the sun as we are distilling it all, bottling it, and (we can always hope) preserving it in the printed word; that we are making a gift to all who read now and to all who may read later.

The best gift is a gift of love—love of life and love of writing. Actually, these two amount to the same thing. The happiest writers, the best writers, seem to me those who love life and writing; who hold two cups, both filled to overflowing, one in each hand, and constantly replenish one from the other.

Ideally, a short story is Life in capsule; the capsule is plot, which may be factory-made. It is a strictly fabricated thing, a mere container. Anybody can make a plot; some writers even manage to sell stories which are nothing but plot. But what kind of gift is an empty capsule? Do editors really prefer buying empty capsules? Do readers prefer reading them?

Let's not bet our writing lives on it! Let's gamble on a surer thing. Let's love life and love writing. Give and give and give. Then, most probably, you will get and get and get. And you needn't feel guilty or uneasy or over-paid, because in this pleasant situation you are always giving more than you're getting. You're giving your heart, and nobody can pay for your heart with mere money. That is as it should be in the matter of gift giving.

All true writing is a gift from you to the rest of the people, whether you know it or not. Given a choice between money and audience, a choice between being paid and being read, I believe even the most calculating writer would settle for being read and let the money go. The fact that being widely read and being well paid go hand in hand today is a very happy circumstance. Not many, if any of us will ever be put to the gruesome test of choosing between money and audience.

This is one of the things that makes writing short stories so satisfying. Think about the pleasant amount of money involved if you should happen to succeed. *But don't think about money while you are actually writing.* If you do, you'll turn in on yourself like a greedy fist, and nothing, absolutely nothing, of any value will come out of you. When you're writing, *write*. Think about money in between times.

If you're just beginning to write short stories, grow them like roses, as a hobby. A hobby leaves you free to experiment and to give your best to the enterprise in joy. It's after you grow a prize winner or two that writing may become a business. But never let the business cramp your freedom to experiment and innovate, to reach out always for the better story you are capable of writing. Don't let business stunt your growth. Don't let it dim your real purpose, which is to grow roses for pleasure and enjoyment, yours and other peoples'—not for hire.

This is tricky to manage, especially right after your first success. Necessarily, you must practice business acumen because there's no getting around it, you are now in business. But you must somehow contrive to be businesslike and at the same time retain the enthusiasm, the innocent charm, the happy non-calculation to which you probably owe your success in the first place.

When at the typewriter or tape recorder or clipboard, whichever you compose on, don't throttle the beautiful pure white goose who laid that first golden egg. In most cases she laid the first one quite inadvertently, and it's no use your choking and squeezing her, hoping this time for an even bigger golden egg. Forget golden eggs and write.

Do enough actual writing (not just talking about it to friends and family) every day so that you don't feel guilty about calling yourself a writer. Play the game often enough so that you're entitled to the name. *Be a writer.*

By this, I don't mean old Wisdom-and-Truth himself, wrapped in flowing robes, holding court. I don't mean the bearded, bourbon hermit in frazzled sweater and slippers, or the odd-ball who devotes himself to living for his art, getting story ideas from knocking around in lowly places, doing lowly things—and then never writing the lowly stories.

To be a writer, all you need is respect for your craft and a few tools exactly as you want them, when you want them.

With some writers it's twenty finely-sharpened pencils and a bushel of yellow sheets. With others it's a typewriter with a new ribbon. For me, it's a tape recorder. Find the best tool for yourself. Keep it in good running order and *use* it.

Time also is a tool, the greatest and the most deceptive. You must use it before it runs away.

Health is another tool, mental and physical health. Don't burn yourself out on one story, even if it is the greatest story ever conceived by man. Save something of yourself for all the other stories you're going to write. Maintain some reasonable balance between killing yourself and being too good to yourself.

Most writers are too good to themselves, but now and then comes a suicidal type. Don't be either. Respect yourself and your craft and your potential future. If you do, you are more likely to command respect from others—the editors, your spouse, your friends, your relatives, even your children.

It is, of course, hardest to command respect from your children, but, in theory, it can be done. Make known to them that you are a writer and that even if they don't understand what a writer is, being one is extremely important to you. Explain to them over and over—with the flat of your hand if necessary—that when you are being a writer, you temporarily cease being a parent. Remind them that they have another parent. Play fair with them, however. When you're not being a writer, be a good parent, a good spouse, a good member of the community, a good citizen.

To take pleasure in writing short stories or writing anything, by all means be good to your *creative* self. Use anything that helps you get the job done more effectively, more quickly, and which isn't unlawful or demoralizing. You must feel like Somebody to write your best. Let it be known around the house that your ego should be treated tenderly, at least until you finish your current piece of copy. If there is no one but you to tend your writer's ego, tend it yourself.

Do anything harmless which will bring out the subconscious you. That's who is doing the biggest part of the writing anyway. But don't use writing as a defense against the world, or as an excuse not to do things which you are morally obligated to do for others, or as a prop for your ego (your ego is a prop for your writing, to be used as such), or for retaliation of a personal nature. Be bitter, be catty, be snobbish, be cruel, insensitive, cold, capricious, ungodly, profane, vicious only within the well defined limits of your characters. Don't use your characters as vehicles for your baser emotions, but as parts of a well thought out, integrated, inevitable whole. If you, the writer, exhibit unpleasant or unpopular attitudes, you may sell once, or in certain times or circles, more than once, but in general I don't think it would be wise to write in this way.

The best examples of fiction writing and the most enduring in the long run, I think, are the stories in which, above and beyond plot, the writer attempted to create more understanding, more sympathy, more compassion among us. Such stories don't come from a writer's grudge-box, but from his heart.

Write from your heart, your soul, your funny-bone, your head—anything but your own private spleen. Write from your pride, if you must—but don't scorn or refuse any legitimate assistance in your endeavor.

You don't refuse the bolts which come to you out of the wild blue yonder, do you? If you have written for any length of time, you know what I mean—the characters, places, situations, themes which come to you from that great Nowhere which all of us are free to draw on, which writers in particular need to draw on.

One of the best ways to pamper your creative self is to feel *big* about your work. Have unbounded confidence in your ability while working and in your unlimited critical qualities when judging what is written. Pretend it's someone else's story you're tearing to shreds! Keep in mind that only the worth of your story will sell it—not your good intentions, your need and desire for money and recognition, or even your connections in the publishing world, if any. Some writers take longer to learn these basic facts than others, but keep trying.

Another thing—don't fight writing. It's like trying to swim by beating at the water. You can't get anywhere that way. Force yourself to believe that writing is a pleasure and a blessing. Actually, it is one of the most penetrating, probing, uplifting, humbling, available therapies in the world—and one of the least expensive.

In the process of creating the right little, tight little world of the slick fiction short story, you may come to see the truth: that it isn't all a trick, that what you're actually doing is making more compatible the world of As-Is with the world of Wish-It-Were, which is something all of us are or should be working toward.

Writing is also the easiest, cheapest road to stardom. You are all the actors, the producer, the director and the stage-set crew; you are a remarkable creature. Enjoy it! Go on and feel remarkable, but don't take yourself too seriously—you are not *that* remarkable. Spend your greatest time and effort making sure the editors take you seriously. Even if you write humorous stories —especially if you write humorous stories—you're going to want the editors to take you seriously and to continue taking you seriously. This means you can't reach a comfortable plateau and just sit there for the rest of your writing life. You must keep growing and getting better.

Make games out of increasing your talent. Everybody has some talent or other to begin with, or he would never have undertaken writing in the first place. The real, the wonderful truth is that all of us have more or less the same potential talent. Some of us simply develop it more fully. Work continually to get the most out of yourself, and I do mean *yourself*. Don't worry about what the other writers are writing, what styles they are using, what fields they're exploiting, what the magazines are buying and printing. Tomorrow they may be buying and printing something entirely different.

Write as you feel, the truth as you see it, and your writing will turn out to be a lot more satisfying than the imitative way and very likely a lot more lucrative, too.

Have a writing schedule, if possible, but don't let it seal you up in a little box. Be flexible. Be *alive*. Learn to write whenever and wherever you can. Work hard and fast and to the best of your ability, and when the opportunity to write is over, give up gracefully. Don't race your motor, don't fume. You're probably beat anyway. Enjoy life for a while. You've earned it.

And there's the trick, if you can manage it. Enjoy

writing tremendously while you're doing it, and when you're not doing it, enjoy life. Life is your reward, always waiting for you outside the closed door.

Now for a final tip. While you're enjoying your re-ward, while you're living it up, there's a little plus-value thing you can be doing: Deep down inside, you can be relating your writing to what's going on—the feel of the water against your skin, the sun, the sky, the taste of food in your mouth, the light through the dining room window, the cries of the children at play, the fat girl in the red swim suit, the smell of chlorine, the strum of your own blood through your veins—relating and digesting and building toward that next writing session.

Now you are living and making stories at the same time. You have finally arrived. One of these days you are going to write the story we all dream of writing, the story which comes out real and urgent—perhaps as clear and complete and thrilling as those two bird calls you heard the other day, one questioning, the other answering. Nature has already written all the stories many times over, but who else but you can bottle and preserve, for a while anyway, those two bird calls, question and answer? *You* can, if you are good enough.

Getting good enough can be joy instead of torture. Just keep in mind at all times that what you're doing is telling the truth as you see it, in an easy-to-swallow-and-digest capsule form. Never forget that the truth as you see it is the thing most likely to make your readers laugh and cry. Some of your truths will make some of them laugh; some of your truths will make some of them cry, but some day, with a single story, you may make all of them laugh and cry at one and the same time, and that will be your day. Work toward it, always aware that writing is only what you make it. Make it rich with satisfaction for yourself. No one else will do this for you!

$\mathcal{T}wo$

ONE HUNDRED AND TWO SELF-STARTERS

Now let's all write a story!

As you have probably begun to understand by now, writing is a state of mind, a way of life in itself. *A short story is for the duration of its composition your way of life,* so if you're going to be stuck with it, you may as well enjoy it.

The first thing you need is an idea, an idea that strikes sparks off your fancy, an idea that you feel compatible with, one that you violently wish to write in such a way that all others will read with alert enjoyment, with awakened understanding, with laughter and tears. You want to stir your readers as they have never been stirred before.

The more violently you wish to write it, the better for your story idea in the long run. As I have said before, plot is not story. Plot is only the capsule, remember. The container. Therefore, don't start with plot, with the mechanics, but with a living idea. Become obsessed with this idea. Then, and only then, should you

16

proceed to story structure and form (call it plot if you like). An ideal story idea, fitted to you and your capabilities, a story idea which obsesses you, creates its own structure and form.

This may sound like putting the cart before the horse, but if you will follow me, I think you will see that to write your best story, you must begin with an idea.

You have no ideas at the moment? Well, let's stir up some. They are there a-plenty, down in your subconscious. The following exercises are designed to bring up at least one and probably a dozen ideas where you can get at them and use them.

Please, for your own benefit, do these on paper, in order and without skipping. Write down your first thoughts quickly and without self-consciousness. Don't just think them—*write them down*. If this sounds like kindergarten, beware!

1. In two short sentences describe an automobile accident as it appears to the driver while it happens. *You* are the driver.

2. One sentence. Describe from your own viewpoint an old man taken completely by astonishment.

3. One sentence. You are an eight-year-old only child. Your new baby sister has just come home from the hospital. How do you feel?

4. You are seventy-seven years of age. Your husband or wife of fifty-eight years has just died. One sentence to express your true anguish.

5. In one sentence give the heart of a scene of natu-

ral violence—a tornado or hail storm in which you are caught out in the open.

6. In one very short sentence, make me smell the fragrance of old-fashioned red roses on a humid, windless, moonlight summer night.

7. Three short lines of meaningful dialogue between a man and wife, quarreling violently.

8. Describe the taste of anger in one word. The scent of sadness in a phrase. The taste of apple in a phrase. The aroma of coffee in a phrase.

9. You are a woman no longer in love with your husband. You are returning his amorous, good-night kiss. Tell me how you feel in one sentence.

10. In one sentence, make the reader feel true nostalgia.

11. You are a man just fired from a well-paying job you hate. How do you feel? Two sentences.

12. You are a young mother. You have just run over your children's puppy in the driveway. How do you feel? One sentence.

13. You are looking directly into the face of a shy, sweet, middle-aged woman who has just been informed that her flower arrangement has won first prize at the Garden Club Show. Describe her face in one sentence.

14. The smile of a martyr in one short sentence.

15. You don't like dogs or cats. While visiting friends who love both, you discover that a flea has attached itself to your ankle. What do you do? One sentence.

16. You are a woman of thirty-eight, snagged on the moment of realization that you have fallen in love

with a no-good man. How do you feel? Two sentences.

17. You are a very beautiful woman; you have just learned that your husband has been unfaithful. Give your first reaction in two short sentences.

18. You are a ten-year-old girl. You are being spanked hard for something you didn't do. How do you feel? One short sentence.

19. You are a forty-year-old woman to whom no man has ever proposed marriage or otherwise. Your face is ugly but your figure is superb. You are toweling off after taking a shower one hot evening and look up to see a man staring in through the open bathroom window. What is your very first unguarded reaction? One sentence.

20. You are a young father seeing your first-born for the first time. One sentence to describe your feelings.

21. Three short meaningful interchanges of dialogue between a pickpocket and his alerted victim.

22. The sound of an egg frying in butter. A phrase.

23. The sound of fist against flesh and bone, in a phrase.

24. One of your acquaintances is a man capable of murder but unaware of it. Describe him. Make the reader know him in two sentences.

25. Write a provocative three-sentence opening paragraph which would make the reader very much want to read the rest of your story.

26. You are a man who does not hate but does not love a woman completely in love with you. Tell her the truth in two short sentences.

27. By physical description alone, show that a char-

acter in your story is completely untrustworthy. One sentence.

28. By physical description only, make the reader know a vulgar person, male or female, in one sentence.

To help you understand what this mental workout is going to do for you, I would like to say that these exercises are designed not only to stir up story ideas, but, in the interest of speedy thought and work habits, to speed up the creative process; to help you learn to invent on the spot what you need; to help you get the most out of the story you choose to write; to improve and develop your dramatic impact.

A short story is necessarily, by virtue or fault of length, only bits and pieces of life, the brightest and the darkest. To be droning and monotonous and undramatic in a short story is unforgivable. Your goal is to make your reader laugh and/or cry. The only way you can make him do either is to startle him out of himself.

The surest, quickest way to startle your reader out of himself is first to startle your own subconscious into active being. You must catch it unawares. That's why I ask that you write these exercises down on paper as quickly as you can without taking second thought or time to become self-conscious. If you stop to think, to become shy, or to become angry with me for asking the impossible of you—that you be in one moment a ten-year-old child enduring a spanking and, in the next moment, a seventy-seven-year-old lady whose husband has just died—you will never find the child or the old lady, both of whom are in you.

Let's continue.

29. Picture a badly scarred woman, without money or prestige, being proposed to by a handsome, healthy man with plenty of money and prestige, who swears he cannot live without her. Why can't he? What is your story explanation of this? As few words as possible.

30. In one sentence show the feeling of a young girl falling in love for the first time.

31. By physical description alone, make the reader see in two sentences the character of a middle-aged woman who is in love with herself.

32. In one sentence sum up an old, old person's feeling about death.

33. You are a young mother and your child is in terrible danger. In one sentence, give your first reaction.

34. You are a forty-eight-year-old man, a successful salesman but getting ulcers. In two sentences describe your hangover the morning after you have taken out a party of important clients whom you despise.

35. Describe, in physical terms only, a happy home that you see in passing. One sentence.

36. In two sentences make the reader feel and know vicious rivalry between two women over a man.

37. In one sentence, from your own viewpoint, show a man and a woman deeply in love after ten years together.

38. In one sentence. You are a teen-aged boy about to take your first driving lesson. How do you feel?

39. From the viewpoint of the jealous one, male or female, show the reader supreme jealousy, in one punchy sentence.

40. In a phrase, make the reader feel spring grass under bare feet on a sunny afternoon.

41. In one sentence each, describe three mouths—a stingy mouth, a greedy mouth, the mouth of a pretty young girl in love.

42. In one sentence, a scream of terror heard late at night in a nice neighborhood.

43. Three provocative short lines of dialogue between a jealous man and his wife who doesn't know that he knows all.

44. You are a nineteen-year-old football tackle. Tell how you would feel if you woke in the night and found your face wet with tears. Two sentences.

45. Inhale the scent of warm ripe cantaloupe and describe it in one short sentence.

46. The feel of salt water on the skin after you emerge from it onto the sunlit beach. One short sentence.

47. In one sentence describe an unusual voice.

48. One tasteful sentence describing honest desire (man for woman or vice versa) from the viewpoint of the one who feels desire.

49. One sentence. The feel of clean socks or hose going on your feet.

50. Describe in one sentence a sound, any sound you choose, heard on a bitter cold, windless morning. In one sentence, the same sound on a hot humid afternoon.

51. Give a living example of pride. Make the reader know pride in one short meaningful sentence.

52. In a phrase, make the reader feel the moonless dark of a summer evening.

53. In a phrase, the taste of a new lipstick just applied.

54. One sentence of dialogue. An inarticulate man declaring his love for a woman.

55. One sentence of dialogue. A fortune hunter declaring his love.

56. A man gives up the woman he loves. Tell one reason for this that might make a story. One sentence.

57. Make the reader feel true embarrassment, in one sentence, from your own viewpoint.

58. In one long sentence, tie up the sound of a fine china cup breaking with the breaking of a heart.

59. In one sentence, describe one potential relationship between rescued and rescuer.

60. You are a fourteen-year-old boy; it is a hot summer afternoon and you have nothing to do. In one sentence make the reader feel your terrible boredom.

61. You are in a hospital. You have just had a serious operation. It is the first day that visitors are permitted in your room. The visiting hour has come, but no visitors. How do you feel? Two short sentences.

62. You are seventy-three years old and live alone in a small apartment. Your only son had promised to come by to see you this afternoon. The afternoon is almost gone and your son has not come. One sentence. How do you feel?

63. You are filling the children's Christmas stockings; you are discovered in the act. What is your initial reaction? Two sentences.

64. You are looking into the face of someone so full of blind hate that he or she does not know what he is doing. Describe the face and your feeling about it in two short sentences.

65. You live in a neighborhood of young couples with very small children. You own the only private swimming pool on your block. You hear one of your

next-door neighbors frantically calling her inquisitive two-year-old. Looking out you see that someone has left the gate unlocked in the enclosure around your pool. The gate is ajar. There is no one in sight, inside or outside the enclosure. You rush out and to the side of the pool. In one sentence, describe your feelings just before you look into the water.

66. You look out your front window and see a leopard padding down your street. What is your first reaction? One sentence.

67. You are going through some old letters and suddenly discover that you are reading a passionate, sincere love letter written to your own husband by another woman during the first year of your marriage. What is your initial reaction? Two sentences.

68. You are a fashion model whose livelihood depends upon your physical appearance. You own two things you care for greatly, a mink coat and a white pedigreed poodle. You wake at two o'clock in the morning to find that your apartment is ablaze. What do you do? Save yourself, try to get out with the fur coat, or reach into the basket for the poodle? Your first action, in one sentence.

69. Walking down a crowded city street, you see a face which intrigues you. Describe it in one sentence.

70. You are five years old and visiting your grandmother. In the night a thunderstorm comes up. Describe your terror in two very short sentences.

71. You are a young girl. It's the night before your wedding. Suddenly you know that you can't go through with it. Why not? Two short sentences.

72. You are a young wife. You like your mother-in-law, but she doesn't like you, even though she gives every appearance of doing so. How do you know she really doesn't like you? One sentence describing the give-away.

73. In the evenings you give demonstration parties with the object of selling for a brush, broom and mop company. Three lines of dialogue between you and a door-to-door salesman from another brush, mop and broom company.

74. You are a baby, one year old. Describe the sunlight coming through the window into your crib, falling over your hands.

75. You are usually a nice person. Everyone thinks of you as a nice person. You have just done something despicable. How do you feel? One sentence.

76. You are a man forty-four years old. One of your assistants has just been promoted over you and is now your boss. Two sentences to describe how you feel the first time you must take direct orders from him.

77. Describe an Indian summer afternoon in one strong sentence.

78. In one sentence of description show that it is Monday without ever stating so.

79. Put your reader right in the middle of a New Year's Eve dance at a small-town country club, in four short sentences.

80. Make me feel a rock 'n' roll beat. One short sentence. (Any rock 'n' roll beat; they all seem alike.)

81. Place your reader unmistakably in a new car by olfactory description only.

82. Describe a truly good person by physical description alone. Two sentences.

83. You are kneading yeast dough on a floured board. Make the reader feel it with you. One sentence.

84. Picture a deserted, rain-wet, small-town main street at night and make the reader see it, too, with a feeling of sadness. Two sentences.

85. In a sentence, give one gesture or one action of an old man who has been a farmer most of his life.

Now let's take a breather and check up on ourselves. Are you enjoying this? If you aren't, it could be that you have what is so aptly known as a writing block. Frankly, I think most writing blocks are just a resistance to getting down to work.

There are genuine blocks, of course. We are all full of quirks and foibles and Freudian tricks. The important thing is to make all this work for us. These exercises are hopefully intended to accomplish just that. What you have actually been doing is stirring up, forcing into the light, the various people contained within yourself, within your imagination and experience.

You have been studying yourself. After all, you are the best subject you'll ever have to study. Learn to be objective about it. Try to catch yourself unawares. There's your gold mine in writing.

The truth is that we are all different, but we're all pretty much alike, too. One thing that keeps a lot of us from writing truly great entertainment is that we're ashamed and worried because we think nobody else ever feels the way we do. Don't worry, don't be ashamed; we're all pretty much the same basic animal.

On the other hand, there are writers who think their own emotions aren't big enough, so they invent impossibly raw, violent, emotional patterns for their characters. I go on the premise that most of humanity has a great deal of good mixed with the other, which I won't call bad, but which is certainly not good. Most of humanity isn't as prudish as some would have us think, but, by the same token, most of humanity is not as abandoned as some hopped-up writers would have us think.

Don't beat your reader over the head with violent, improbable emotions. He'll most likely get worn out and leave you. You can be much more impressive by lifting your reader out of his chair with one honest, wonderful or terrible thing. *One* terrible or wonderful thing is sufficient for a skillful, honestly written short story. More than three is too much.

Don't be wasteful. Exercise 9, for instance, in which the woman no longer in love with her husband is forced to endure his amorous bedtime kiss, is big enough and terrible enough, if handled properly, to be the high point of an entire short story.

When you finish all the exercises, you will probably find that you are truly interested in only a half-dozen or so. Of these half-dozen, you may find yourself obsessed with only two. Weigh your obsessions and settle for the strongest and most powerful. That will be your story. Throw all the other story ideas out of your mind and let this *one* take you over and grow inside you to its fulfillment.

Now, for those stubborn souls whose subconscious may still be asleep, here is the final section of our mental workout.

86. It's your first night in a strange hotel. You wake at daybreak and don't know where you are. In that first lost moment where do you think you are? Two sentences.

87. Using only physical description, action and gesture, make the reader realize that a woman has been had by the man with her; he is *not* her husband. Two sentences.

88. In one sentence, relate gently falling snow to death from old age.

89. Describe a gesture which gives away a broken heart. One sentence.

90. Relate rain to quiet, secure happiness. One sentence.

91. Show a teen-aged combo playing their first paid engagement. Two sentences.

92. You are a pretty young wife whose feet are slightly on the large side. Your husband of six months has just presented you with a beautiful pair of bedroom slippers one size too small. How do you feel? One sentence.

93. You are a successful young man of thirty-two. Suddenly you find that you hate the woman you love. How can this ambiguous thing be? Describe your feelings, in two sentences. Make the reader understand how you can hate and love at one and the same time.

94. Three sweet, innocent lines of dialogue between

a teen-aged boy and girl on a date; both are having their first date.

95. Four meaningful lines of dialogue between a teen-aged boy and his grandmother, the boy having just discovered that his grandmother is not an old fuddy-duddy, after all.

96. Relate the making of a decision, a hard decision, with the feeling of water closing over your head. One sentence.

97. Your best friend moved to another state last week. You inadvertently passed his or her house at dinnertime, just at sundown. The house is still unoccupied. How did you feel? One sentence.

98. You are incurably ill of some disease or other. You realize that your youngest child, twelve years of age, has found out your secret. What do you say to the child in your first moment of realization? Two lines of dialogue.

99. At a wedding reception, two maiden aunts of yours, strict teetotalers, are getting tipsy on the vodka-spiked punch. How do you tell them? Two lines of dialogue. (You are the one who spiked the punch.)

100. In one discreet, subtle, tasteful sentence, show by physical description and tell-tale action that someone is a homosexual.

101. One valid circumstance in which a man, very much in love with his wife, murders her.

102. One phrase each: a bitter smile; a forlorn smile; a brave smile; a challenging smile; a tender smile; an insincere smile.

It is in the climate of enforced quiet and rest and meditation after stimulation that stories are born. It was to set up your own story climate that I put you through the above self-starters. Don't be alarmed if the story idea you're now tingling with isn't among those I've flung at you. But *do* be alarmed if you're not tingling! If at this moment you don't have a single story idea, either directly from the preceding exercises or one of your own plucked from the exhaust fumes of creative stimulation, then it will take more power than I profess to blast away the solid rock in which you've hidden your natural creative ability.

But if you are tingling with a story idea, take a meditation break. You deserve it; you need it. Now that your subconscious is awake and working, now that you have allowed yourself to be possessed by and obsessed with a story idea, you want to write the story. You want to rush to the typewriter and put it all down, willy-nilly, any old way. You're trembling with eagerness and bravado and fear. You want to *see* this brain child. You want to deliver it *now,* at whatever cost to you or the brain child!

If you persist in writing your story at this early stage, it won't be good for you or your brain child. *Don't rush things.* This is the one period in writing a story in which speed is no asset, in which haste makes waste. At least, such has been my experience. Allow the story to grow naturally. You have brought your idea up out of your subconscious; the light of your conscious is shining on it, but it is still just a seed. *Leave it where it belongs.* Let it go through all the processes it must.

A note of caution: Don't, however, let your story idea

stay underground too long. Don't be afraid when the moment comes (and you will know when that is) to allow your story to sprout. If you wait too long, if you are afraid, the seed may rot.

Make notes during the germination time. Jot down things you may want to use in this particular story, that you think you may need—bits of dialogue, key words which will bring a character, a whole scene, alive for you later. If not used in this story, they can always be used in another, for you're not going to write only one story; remember, you're going to write many stories.

There are many methods of germinating successfully and at a high pitch. Take long walks in the rain. Sit alone and listen to music with your clipboard and paper and pencil handy. You may even fit the mood of the music with the mood of the story you want to do.

The germination period is the time when your idea begins putting on flesh. In the germination period, this is mainly for *your* benefit. If you can't see your characters in action, if you can't smell them and hear them and watch them move, your reader will never be able to. The more clearly and truly you see the characters in your own story, the closer you will come to creating a climate which will enable your reader to see them clearly and truly later on.

While your story is still germinating, you can consider what type of story it is that you have gotten hold of. By that, I mean what type of story it is in relation to you, the would-be creator. I see three basic creative wellsprings from which all stories flow. The first is Personal Experience—the idea based on a personal experience which, considered as a story, lacks either beginning, middle, or end. This you must supply.

Secondly, there is Personal Emotion which you transpose, sublimate, and re-fit into a story idea. You may get the idea first and furnish it with your own emotion. Or you may feel the emotion so strongly that you create the story idea as a vehicle for it.

Thirdly, there is the story you get, seemingly, from Out of Nowhere—a story handed to you out of the blue, without your even asking for it. In fact, *not* asking is the best way I know to attract an Out-of-Nowhere story! Actually, it doesn't come from nowhere; nothing comes from nowhere. It comes from so deep in your subconscious, your racial and human heritage, that you cannot recognize it as something known to you.

The Personal Experience Story. The Personal Emotion Story. The Out-of-Nowhere Story. Decide during the germination period which wellspring your story comes from. Knowing what you are doing and what you are up against, your strong points and your possible weaknesses in writing this particular story, knowing the nature of the beast, will give you confidence. Knowledge in this case, as in most cases, is infinitely better than ignorance.

Some of you may never write any but the completed Personal Experience. That's fine. Some of the best stories are such. Some of you will write only Personal Experience and Personal Emotion. Again, that's fine. The same goes for those who write nothing but Out-of-Nowhere Stories. There is some slight advantage in being able to write all three kinds (or, even, a three-in-one!), but if you write only one or two kinds, don't worry about it. There is no particular merit in one type of story over the others.

Since I have arbitrarily divided creative well-springs and their products into these three types, the most helpful way I can illustrate them is with my own stories. Aside from a certain lack of modesty, which writers tend toward, I use my own stories because I know them best. In using them, I will be more likely to take you behind the veil of creation. I say "likely" because however much any writer may wish to take others behind the veil of his own creation, no matter how fluent or persuasive he may be, it is, in a complete sense, impossible. But I will do my best.

Three

THE PERSONAL EXPERIENCE STORY

ALL you need for the Personal Experience Story is a personal experience, plus a burning desire to translate it into something a lot of people will read with enjoyment, *after* an editor has paid you for it. And don't tell me you've never had an interesting personal experience. Everybody has thousands! What about the day the power mower went berserk? Remember the evening of the bat? The time you dropped your car keys through the grating? The morning you thought Junior drank nail polish remover? You can do better without half trying, can't you?

Actually, it doesn't have to be much of an experience, but it sure had better be *personal,* intimate, with meaning and value to you, because you are the one, and only one, who can select and add to and take away from and keep the precious breath of life in this fictionized version of what happened to you. *Fictionized*—never neglect that element of it.

I have written and sold stories inspired by a pet sparrow, a very small automobile accident, and other more intimate incidents in my life. But without the catalytic application of *fiction* to these incidents, they would have been, at best, mere sketches and slices, bits and pointless pieces of life—and, at worst, plain boring!

Life without fiction, just as surely as fiction without life, makes for a ho-hum story (or no story at all). Your personal experience is worth little, if anything, unless and until you are able to lift out of yourself, the loose and often tedious fabric of real life and work it over according to the stern (but never rigid!) structural and dramatic dictates of fiction.

To illustrate briefly: The story inspired by our pet sparrow ("The Sparrow's Mother," *Redbook,* April, 1960) whom we raised almost from the egg and who was with us for two years before her passing, would have been no more than an *account* of a delightful little scold who lived out her last year with one crooked leg, one stump, and a ferocious amount of will power and gallantry. But how many people are interested in the history of a sparrow from cradle to grave? More importantly, how many fiction editors buy *accounts* of sparrows to fill their short story pages?

The fictionizing trick here was to make the sparrow serve a definite, dramatic purpose within a definite story structure. The story, as I eventually wrote it, was composed of many small personal-experience bits derived from my children, their playmates and their pets. But every bit of it served the story (the plot, the container), which was *fiction*—which I, the writer, had to supply!

The small automobile accident was easier ("Did You Have A Good Day, Mary Kim?" *Family Circle,* December, 1958). All I did here was give the true sequence of that awful day a few brushstrokes of fiction's gold (including a blonde rinse for myself, and the lopping off of a few cumbersome years!) and refute the practical, good-wife, real life ending in favor of the delightful, irresponsible ending I had come close to supplying, anyway!

To illustrate the Personal Experience Story in more detail I have chosen "Tiger in the Living Room" (*Cosmopolitan,* July, 1956). I chose it over several others with more personal experience detail because it seems that more husbands than not have the habit of falling asleep after dinner, even on occasions such as wedding anniversaries.

That, in its universal simplicity, is the Personal Experience which moved me sufficiently to begin writing the story in my mind while the experience was occurring, and later that same evening, to type the beginning. I finished the story the next morning. The way it was originally written is substantially the way it appeared in the magazine.

The germination period for "Tiger in the Living Room" took place before the story idea ever occurred to me, oddly enough and yet not so oddly considering the classic nature of the situation. My husband had already fallen asleep after so many, many dinners and on so many important (to me) occasions, that the germination had occurred without my realizing it.

On the evening in question, his turning up his toes and his nose, and going off to sleep, produced in me a heated frenzy which burst the seed covering and suddenly there was the sprout; the story itself burst into full growth in the tropical climate of my anger. I was completely without cleverness or artifice. I wrote:

"Wake up, wake up, Mr. Hughes! I'm asking you, I'm warning you. . . . I'm begging you. There's something dangerous in this room. Can't you feel it, even through those layers of after-dinner insulation? It's a tiger thing. Once—I don't recall how many months and years ago—it was small; it could be picked up like a kitten and put out for the night. But it's grown and grown. Now it's even bigger than *you* and that frightens me.

"It would frighten you, too, if you woke up suddenly and discovered it here in the living room. Except that if you woke up it would go away, I think. I'm not so sure anymore, but I think it would."

I meant every word I wrote, and that fact, plus the fact that every word was written at white heat, was the thing which sold this story, I'm sure, for it is a very, very slim story. Not on the surface a story at all, just a man asleep on a couch and his wife sitting looking at him. No props to speak of, no visitors, and all of it in the wife's mind. It isn't very long, but on the other hand, it isn't a short-short, and re-reading it now, seeing it in print in a magazine—such a slim little thing all in a woman's mind with nothing to recommend it but the true white heat with which it was written—I am very proud to have written it, to have spoken for all women, and even prouder to have sold it. Even a busy editor must have recognized that though the entire story happened in the heroine's mind, all the elements of story are present: the "gimmick", the problem, the various attempts to resolve it, the tentative solutions, the rending decision point, and, finally, the two faces—one dark, one bright—of the reward for having made the hard *good* decision.

Now for the rest of the story in telescope form. The oblivious sleeping husband and the lady, very wakeful. "It's very dangerous, this tiger that prowls our living room. . . . It's dangerous and the most dangerous thing about it is, it's *me*. You didn't know you married a tiger? Well, you didn't, because I wasn't a tiger at the time, seven years ago. *Exactly* seven years ago. Our anniversary. *Salud,* Mr. Hughes, and many happy returns! At least you don't sleep with your mouth open. You sleep like a little boy. . . . But what do I care? Tigers don't need love; tigers don't love. That's what makes them dangerous."

The lady has already made a decision of sorts. "I'm not going to hit you with this heavy snow-scene-under-glass paper weight your Uncle Foster gave you on your third birthday. I'm not even going to wake you rudely by shouting and crying. . . . It's too late. I sit here calmly, this tiger me, and look at you with dry, dispassionate wonder. The big upended feet. Hands clasped over your tummy—you're getting one, did you know? And that innocent, boyish face. *What did I ever see in you, Mr. Hughes?* So long ago, that time of mating. . . . It was someone else, Mr. Hughes, not you. You can't possibly be that agile Pan who piped his springtime tune in the campus sunken garden. Where did it go, the forever-and-ever song of love?"

The lady is filled with soured hope. "There we sat at the table, just you and I, because I'd fed the children early. Garlic bread, sirloin, green salad, king-size chocolate cake, and I in my second-best dress. And you. . . . Under all that hair I thought I saw two little roundy humps pushing up where your horns used to be. He *remembers,* I thought. . . . I just wanted you to remember, that was all. You remember things all the time, when to have the oil changed in the car, when to pay your insurance premiums, when the Marilyn Monroe movie is on. Is it too much to ask that you remember the day you acquired your cook-housekeeper-laundress and the mother of your children? *Is it?* Yes, it is too much to ask of you, Mr. Hughes. I can see it now. Else you couldn't lie there bloated with sleep while I suffer! "We're telepathic to each other," you once said. Or did I say it to you? It doesn't matter because we were. Telepathic. . . . "When he stops being telepathic to me," I told myself wisely, "then I'll know it's ended." Of course, I didn't think it would ever end, but it has. Our love, Mr. Hughes, is stone-cold dead in the market place. Like the open-eyed fish in their nests of ice. Gelid. And who killed the beautiful darting fish? *You,* Mr. Hughes. . . . This is your last chance! Either you rise up and acknowledge our seventh wedding anniversary, within the next *five minutes,* or I am going to. . . . Well, I am going to leave you, Mr. Hughes. . . . Please, Mr. Hughes, this is serious. In three and a half minutes you will lose your cook-housekeeper-laundress. . . . If you don't wake in two minutes and say, "Happy anniversary wife!" I am going to rise from my crouching position in this chair and glide noiselessly

out that door and never come back. . . . Of course I'm
taking the children. You don't think I'd leave them
with you? I'd hesitate to trust a horned toad to your
care. What will I use for money? Don't underestimate
my resources, Mr. Hughes. . . . I'm rich. There's a
week's grocery allowance in my red purse. . . . The
way I see it, that money is mine. When it's gone, I'll get
a job. . . . Remember, that first year we were married
I worked in Mr. Hewitt's office. . . . That first apartment, so tiny it's a wonder I didn't discover then we
were incompatible. . . . How nice if we had been
compatible, Mr. Hughes. . . . Sorry, time's up. I am
sorry, believe it or not. . . . To tell the truth, Mr.
Hughes, I'll probably miss you. Like the ache when a
bad tooth is pulled. . . . I'll bet next year you'll remember our anniversary! Now that I'm actually leaving, how helpless you look lying there. Maybe it's only
because you skipped your haircut, but you look so
frayed, so spent. I really am going to miss you; it wasn't
all dull and tedious. . . . Sometimes when you
weren't sleeping. . . . You know what? I'm going to
kiss you. A light, quick one. . . . One for the road, Mr.
Hughes. One for the long, lonesome road. *Salud, auf
Wiedersehen* and happy dreams, Mr. Hughes. I really
mean it. Even the tiger—

"Why, Mr. Hughes, I only brushed you with my lips,
but you're . . . *awake.* Looking up at me out of clear
green-gray eyes—they really are green-gray with iri-
descent flecks like tiny darting fish. Now you're holding me, so close that the newspaper on your tummy rat-
tles like dried palm leaves. . . . You're kissing me! Oh,
what a hash I've made of leaving you! This is so embar-

rassing, Mr. Hughes—and so wonderful. Celebrate? What exactly, precisely, do you wish to celebrate, Mr. Hughes? Oh. You just feel like celebrating. You know what? I have just made a momentous decision. I am going to *forget* our anniversary. What's a wedding anniversary anyway? Just a date on a calendar, that's all. Guess what I'm going to celebrate, Mr. Hughes? *You.* Remembered or present, dull or scintillating, asleep or awake! That dratted tiger! Actually, if it weren't for the tiger, I wouldn't have decided to leave you and I wouldn't have kissed you the way I did, without rancor or bitterness; you wouldn't have waked up and we wouldn't—"

Now do you see what I mean about the Personal Experience story? It has the advantage of being written out of emotions so strong that they can carry even a slim story with little or no physical action. One definite pitfall is that you may not be able to avoid writing in all the personal detail (such as names and ages of children, descriptions of several other similar evenings, husband's job, etc.) which would drag on the classic story situation and diffuse the lady's wrath to the point where it was no longer compelling. Omit everything in the Personal Experience story which belongs only in your cluttered memory. Use only those personal details and emotions which further the story as a story.

Fictionize.

Dramatize.

Watch out for tedium as you would watch out for snakes. After all, you are prowling around in your own underbrush. You may love every remembered leaf and twig of it, but you can bet your reader won't. He's got plenty of underbrush of his own to brood upon, lovingly, in spare moments. He won't be interested in your memories (unless, of course, you happen to be Duke or Duchess, King or Queen, or the kid who sat on the tip of a flagpole for six weeks, and even those accounts are usually—look closely—highly fictionized, if not in content, in presentation). Your memories aren't worth a nickel unless you trim them down, dress them up, and organize them in some sort of container.

Real life seldom makes short stories for you; it merely provides the raw material, the wellsprings, the whole cloth on which you, the writer, place your little pattern. And then you cut! You cut like mad, every last dear (to you) thing which has no place in your story. You substitute and change and improvise with absolute care and ruthlessness, for at this point the wellspring has done its work. Your personal experience, as such, has lost its importance.

What if you were ten years old when this strange and wonderful thing happened to you? The editors will like your story much better if you change your age to twenty-one! You were fifty-three and gray-haired when the prowler broke into your bedroom? Make yourself twenty-nine with a lustrous chestnut mane. So what if I didn't actually own a snow scene paperweight to throw at my sleeping husband, didn't have a week's grocery allowance in my purse (not red, either), and didn't really make such definite plans to leave him—so what? The truth is no more—the story's the thing, and you're writing it!

Four

THE PERSONAL EMOTION STORY

THE Personal Emotion Story is really nothing but a rarefaction of the Personal Experience Story. The difference is that your Personal Experience Story most often springs directly from physical circumstances and occurrences which are reconstituted, largely, in the story you write. Not so with Personal Emotion. In this type of story, *all* you carry over is the emotion. You may use it to furnish and heat a big bare house of story plot you already have. Or you may wish so strongly to communicate the emotion that you create a story simply as a vehicle for it.

Most love stories, and I would say all the best ones, are Personal Emotion, not Personal Experience. You either love, or remember love, or wish to love, and if you are that strange, shy, lonely, grand creature who is a writer, you pour this personal emotion into a container which will show it off to fullest advantage and at the same time keep your secret for you.

This is also done with the other strong personal emotions: hate, desire, compassion, anger, lust, grief. In each case, the *emotion* is the source of the story. You may have been suffocatingly in love with little Suzie Ketchum when you were twelve, and by the same token you violently hated your rival, Ronald Morningham, but Suzie and Ronald, even their names, are gone now into the mists of time; only the emotions, *your* young love and *your* young hatred, remain. Even if you have never felt an emotion since (highly unlikely!), you know about love and hate. You're in business. All you need are some good eye-catching containers. If, like most of us, you have suffered and enjoyed all the major emotions, and have continued through the years to suffer and enjoy them in all their variants and refinements, your cup runneth over!

One of the great advantages of the Personal Emotion Story over the Personal Experience Story is that the emotional wellspring seldom runs dry. From the same source you can produce innumerable stories, each a standout in its own right, whereas the specific personal experience yields only one—or, at the most, several stories for even the most cunning and thrifty of writers.

The thing I really like about writing the Personal Emotion Story is that it demands more artistry than carpentry. The cart, the container, the plot, is *behind* the horse (the good old four-legged, moving force—the emotion, if you will) where it rightly should be. The only dangers here are that you may choose a cart too heavy and cumbersome for your horse to pull, or one so fragile that the silly little vehicle may be dashed to pieces before you reach your destination. Otherwise, the trip is wonderful!

To illustrate the Personal Emotion Story I am going to use "He Went Home Early," published in the February, 1955 issue of *Redbook*.

The impetus for this story came from loving my husband very much and knowing that he loved me, but realizing that the whole thing was getting a little frayed around the edges because his job was consuming most of his time and energy. I couldn't seem to find the words when we were together, to let him know that I understood all this—that I still loved him and knew that he still loved me, that it was only the job getting in our way, the quite necessary, oh, very fiendishly necessary job which brought in the money that paid our keep.

I became obsessed with the idea of writing it in such a way that he would know I understood. With the dubious two-edged intelligence of professional fiction writers, I could see no better way to do it than to incorporate it into a story which might sell to a magazine. This is not quite so mercenary a thing as it may seem at first glance. Even the best of husbands have to be roused to attention. What better way to get my own husband's attention than to write a story that a magazine would publish and pay money for? In other words, if it were published, he would have to read it. He would find the time somehow. I wasn't so sure about his finding the time to read a declaration of love and understanding in the form of a personal note.

Furthermore, I decided a story would be easier to write. And there is a curious thing which happens to people who write: Sooner or later, you will probably find that you are communicating with those you love and like, and perhaps even those you hate, through your stories. This isn't so bad a thing. Actually, it's good—good for you and very good for your writing. When you put your big emotions on paper in the form of stories, you, at one and the same time, clarify, intensify, and discipline. Nothing on earth can suffer from clarification, intensification, and discipline. Certainly your writing can't!

In "He Went Home Early," I first thought, naturally, of doing it from the wife's point of view. But that would express only *love* in depth; I wanted *understanding* in depth. Therefore, I decided to write it from the husband's point of view.

(Incidentally, if your writing suffers from diffuseness, I would suggest your using the viewpoint of the opposite sex. Try it for a story which keeps getting lost on the sidings. I hope it works as well for you as it does for me.)

You may think this was a very strange gift to make for my husband—to write a story from *his* viewpoint showing how much he loved *me*, his wife! But think about it. Wasn't this the best way to show that I loved him—by showing that I knew and understood that he still loved me, that it was only the press of his job which prevented his being more demonstrative about it? By writing the story from his viewpoint, I could also avoid the danger of the fuzzy diffuseness and overwriting which are too often peculiar to the woman's viewpoint story as written by a woman.

The instant I decided on the husband's point of view,

the story almost wrote itself, which is always a thrilling thing.

Now for a telescoped version of the story to illustrate the points which I have tried to make.

Preston Aircraft's new fighter-bomber proposal had been accepted in Washington. Everybody was grinning and talking. Matthew Graham stood half-in, half-out of his private office, watching things go to pieces. There were already a few spiked Cokes being circulated. By three o'clock, there wouldn't be a clear eye in the place, except for his own and those of a couple of middle-aged secretaries. He let them go home. And then he was sitting there in the quiet. Suddenly he felt the weight of all the other days, the evenings and the nights he had spent in this place. He realized he didn't want to work. Even his hand—he stared at it with resentment and then with curiosity—was refusing to curl around his pencil. He hated sitting here like the last survivor of some lost civilization.

Aloud, he uttered the short, explicit, masculine word that he used maybe twice a year. It echoed flatly in the silence, reminding him of the Sunday morning when the plaster fell off the dining-room ceiling into his coffee, and he said the word in front of the children. He remembered the way his wife had looked at him—that straight-on, thoughtful look that had left him feeling she knew all there was to know about him, while he knew nothing about her.

Filled with a curious anger, he got his hat and his raincoat and walked out. It had been raining when he came to work this morning. But now the sky was a soft, washed blue. Like the inside of a cup, he thought, and then he wondered why he had thought of a cup. He was filled with a sudden, shameful exhilaration to be idling when everyone, even the children in their schoolrooms, was hard at work. As he drove, he stared from side to side at the unfamiliar world. A world of women.

He was reminded of his wife and what she had said to him this morning—or was it last week?—about the power mower. He was supposed to have it fixed. He felt a sudden tightening in his throat—a warm, anticipatory sense of haste. His foot pressed down hard on the gas pedal. And then it lifted. Lin didn't know he was coming home.

Coming into the town that Lin had chosen because it was a good place for the children, the small, quiet, weather-beaten Texas town that was still strange to him after—was it really three years?—he slowed the car to a walk.

"You can't really belong and be a part of." Lin's voice—something she had said to him when they moved here. "It isn't your fault. It just means that, on account of the children, I will have to belong double and be two parts of." She had said it calmly, dispassionately. But now he remembered the soft, vulnerable look of her neck, the unprotected little hollow at the base of it with her pulse beating swiftly. If she had known how it was going to be, would she have chosen this—this double belonging, this being two parts of?

It struck him that he no longer had any knowledge of his wife. In the beginning it had seemed to him that he knew her. Where had it all gone? Now there was only the hasty tumult of breakfast, the slightly more subdued tumult of dinner when he was able to make it, the short hours of sleep in the same bed. She was always against twin beds. He felt himself warm a little. But was Lin still against twin beds? He didn't know.

All of a sudden, time seemed to swirl about him, multi-colored ribbons on a Maypole, and he was the pole with the bright ribbons wrapping him 'round and 'round while he stood stiff and unbending in the center, smothered by time's passing. The daylight hours— those were the ones. If a man worked nights, for instance—

"He works the night shift out at the plant." Lin's voice in his mind again. "That's all right for a bachelor, I suppose, and it was good to have a man around this afternoon when the grass caught fire on Portinger's vacant lot. . . ."

Chris Vance. Matt remembered now. He had seen him coming out of the apartment house next door. Whistling. Oh, the fellow had every reason to whistle! He had all the daylight hours. . . . Time to help Lin put out fires. And just by looking out his window, this Chris Vance could know pretty well what Lin was doing any hour of the day! Maybe he even dropped over for a cup of coffee sometimes. Or a Coke if it was hot like today, and Lin sitting there in those damned short shorts.

Then, turning into his own street, he went sick with shame. He saw the roof of his house and his shame went away, leaving only a faint brassy taste in his mouth. The house was old and planted like a rock. When they had bought it, Lin had had some notion of doing it over. She had wanted a breakfast bar to divide the big old kitchen, but he had never built it. She hadn't mentioned the breakfast bar in a long time.

He saw Lin's old station wagon parked alongside the garage. She was home. Or was she? She had her own life, her own world, and he had his. And that was a lousy, lonely thing to come up against on a sunny afternoon. Instead of going to the side door, he went to the front door. The living room was strange to him without the Sunday funnies strewn about and the kids sprawling, watching television. A woman's room. Carefully, he walked through it, his footsteps echoing. She wasn't home.

And then her voice called, "Is that you, Kate?"

"It's me," he said, letting out his breath.

She was in the little spare room that was papered in big pink roses. "This is my room," she had said when they moved in. Here she was, and she was sewing, a cascade of pale blue cotton stuff falling across her lap and onto the floor. She didn't get up. "You're sick," she said.

"No, I never felt better in my life." Which was a lie, him standing here on the threshold of this virginal little room that was so completely hers that he might never have existed for her at all. She wore a housecoat which buttoned from her throat to the floor with tiny black buttons. With her dark blonde hair pinned up on her small head, she looked—well, "girlish" wasn't the word, but that was the nearest he could come to it.

He had the strange feeling that time had slipped a cog and that none of it had happened—the college courtship, the ten years of marriage. He was back in some other time, and she was the virginal young girl that he loved; at the same time, she was his girl's mother, and he had come to speak for the right to court her daughter. It was curious and confusing, inasmuch as he had never had such a scene with Lin's mother.

Still, the feeling persisted, striking him with such force that it was all he could do to keep from crying out, "You can trust her with me—now and later, to love and cherish for all time!"

Then the illusion passed. "The fighter-bomber proposal was accepted," he said tiredly. "I took the afternoon off. I thought we might do something together." He felt himself flushing. "Of course, you may have plans. You were sewing—"

"Just hemming a dress." Suddenly she turned full around to face him, and he heard the full-throated sound of her laughter in the room. "I'm so glad you came home!"

Relief washed over him—relief and contrition and a great, surging desire to do something for her. "I guess this is a fine opportunity for me to make that breakfast bar you wanted!"

Her teeth showed white under her short, full upper lip. "Oh, yes—the breakfast bar!"

Coming back to the kitchen with the lumber, he put it down and rubbed his hands together, grinning. "I'll have this thing built and installed in time for the kids to eat dinner off it! And what about the mower? I can fix that, too."

"Oh, the mower's fixed," she said. "Chris fixed it last week."

Chris? The name dropped into him like a stone. Sav-

agely, he struck a nail, pounding it in. He lined up another nail. What in hell's wrong with me? But it was
too late for introspection, for just then he hit his
thumb with the hammer, so hard that it started turning blue as he watched. And then he couldn't see for
the pain ballooning in him—he actually wanted to faint
and be done with it. But he couldn't faint because he
didn't want to make himself a bigger fool in front of
his wife than he already was.

She had his hand under the tap, she was splashing
water up on his face, bending around him. "That
was mean of me," she said, low and fierce. "Telling
you Chris fixed the mower. Making a thing of it."

She knew why he had banged his thumb. Forgive
me, he thought. "I'll try to be home more," he said
hoarsely. Forgive—forgive! His arms went around
her before he knew they were going to. Under his wet
hands, he felt the narrow back tapering down to the
incurving waist. "Lin? Lin?" It was his own voice saying her name, urgent, questioning. And her voice answering. "Matt." That low, full syllable of recognition
and acquiescence.

Their room was cool and dim, and the house quiet.
She was so clean, so beautiful, so familiar, and yet so
strange, this wife of his. Her hair was like silk under his
aching thumb, and she was everything soft and yield-
ing. And yet, there was such strength under her yield-
ing that he trembled to think it might ever be turned
against him. . . .

She said it softly, drowsily, into the quiet. "And they
were together and they became one. . . ." The words
touched him with surprise, then with wonder. She has

forgiven me, he told himself. But when he turned his head he saw that she was asleep, her face as still and passionless and unremembering as a child's face. He wanted to lie there forever, watching her sleep. Yet, perversely, he wanted to wake her and tell her again how much he loved her and why he loved her. To tell her again that he would change, that he would be home more, and that things would be different.

Then the telephone rang. She slipped, in one motion, out of sleep and into her robe and was in the hall answering it.

He lay there, hating telephones. She stood in the doorway. "Who was it?" he cried, thinking of the children. "Who was it?"

"It was Kate. She wanted to know why I didn't come to bridge this afternoon. She said she kept waiting and then they had to throw out one table. . . ."

Suddenly it all came flooding in on him again—the shame, the guilt, the knowledge that he had invaded her day, her world, the one she had built to sustain her through the loneliness he imposed upon her—and would go on imposing upon her. For there was no way to make a living now except the way he had chosen.

She was still looking at him in that stunned way. "I could at least have called," she said, "but when you came in, I forgot." A little quiver ran over her face. She was going to cry. . . . Then he saw the bright flash of teeth under her full upper lip. She was laughing! Standing there with one arm flung up against the door frame. Laughing. "One table thrown out. One whole table! And you know what, Matt? The children will be home from school any minute!"

Shocked and undone, he stared at her. Then it hit him—what she had said. "When you came in, I forgot." She had forgotten; he had made her forget, and she wasn't sorry a bit! Suddenly he was laughing, too. Laughing like a happy fool, because, in spite of telephones and bridge and Preston Aircraft and bachelor neighbors and kids coming home from school—in spite of the whole cockeyed set-up, and maybe a little because of it—they had a place, just the two of them, that nothing could get at. And as long as they had it, he would be fine and she would be fine. Everything would be fine.

I would like to point out here that the problem in this story was not solved physically. At the end of the story the physical situation is unchanged. The solution to the problem was an *emotional* one. The change occurred in the hero. He found his courage in honest acknowledgement of fact and in his love for his wife, and in the fact that she returned his love fully. The most powerful and universal problems for short stories, as in life, can never be solved by physical, mechanical means alone. Even in a man-against-nature story, the thing which gives the hero strength to push the boulder away, to kill the man-eating tiger or to swim the alligator-infested river, comes from within the hero. The solution of his problem, in the final analysis, rests with the hero. For that reason you must have real and compelling heroes.

Many writers today (in pursuit of realism, I suppose) use a neat, rather dreary, blended type of hero, neither very good nor very bad in any of his thoughts or actions. Heroes with grey flannel souls. While this may be fine for contemporary fiction, I somehow don't believe it. In the first place, people haven't changed that much. I especially don't believe it is good for fictional purposes.

The most real and compelling heroes (*and* villains) of history, including Biblical history, and many or all of our outstanding heroes (and villains) even today seem to me to have (or have had) two-tone souls! Strong and striking. Embattled.

Imagine your fictional hero's soul as two pieces of torn paper, a portion of purest white, a portion of blackest black, and the two ragged edges overlapping at the center. It is there at the schism and the bridge that your story happens. There is your hero (or will he turn out to be a villain?) caught on his own particular sharp pinpoint of truth, between the hounds of heaven and the black dogs of Lucifer, all of which are kenneled inside himself.

The intensity of man's desire to be good is usually counterbalanced—at some time in his life, if not continually—by an equally intense desire to give in, to give up, to be bad and enjoy it to the fullest! Catch your hero (or villain) there, at the ragged place between white and black, and you have your story. Most likely, a powerful one.

I'm sorry that Matt Graham in the preceding story is not a more vivid illustration of the black-and-white hero. (At the time I wrote this story I had considerably more timidity in such matters than I have now!) But the story as a whole is, I think, a pretty good example of the Personal Emotion Story.

Five

THE OUT-OF-NOWHERE STORY

IF YOU really wanted to, and had the time, you could probably figure out where your Out-of-Nowhere Story came from. You'd end up with an equation, most likely, which cubed and squared and multiplied a lot of wildly irrelevant things—the time you almost drowned when you were six, a blind date when you were seventeen, the smooth lethal feel of your son's latest addition to his rock collection, and your boss's voice saying, "Sorry, Hubert, no raise." Plus the smell of the inside of your great-grandfather's leather collar-bag, and a memory in essence of Dickens' *Martin Chuzzlewit*.

But why bother? Take the Out-of-Nowhere Story for what it is, a boon, an unexpected bonus, manna from writers' heaven, a gift handed to you out of Nowhere, which is really the vast Somewhere of your subconscious, everything you have ever seen, done, felt and smelled, touched, tasted, heard, thought, dreamed, feared and loved, won, lost, imagined, and read. Yes, *read*, for every other writer's writings to date make up part of the reservoir on which we draw. But why pick the source to pieces? Accept the story. *Write it.*

To illustrate the Out-of-Nowhere Story, I'm going to use my "Romance in the Park" which appeared in the March, 1957, issue of *Cosmopolitan*. One evening, I was sitting in the car watching my husband and son play tennis on the courts in our small city park. Our little girl was dashing about under the trees, sometimes disappearing into the shadows near the small creek which runs through the park.

I could hear the jukebox over at the swimming pool and, through the trees, see the yellow low-hung lights of the miniature golf course. I was tired and faintly bored, but compelled to a certain necessary alertness by the small lone figure playing under the big shadowing trees. All of a sudden I felt the park as a preserve, a compound, a small safe lighted area in the vast dark night. What would it be like if a marauder came quietly, stealthily into it, in among all the happy, innocent, ill-prepared people?

And there, suddenly, was my story, based on nothing, handed to me, characters and all.

I wrote it with great joy and abandon because to a hard-working writer there is nothing so delightful as the "free" story, the one without extreme personal involvement. By this, I don't mean that you are freed from getting inside the characters in your Out-of-Nowhere Story; you must get inside your characters, whatever kind of story you write. But in the Out-of-Nowhere Story, it's like putting on masks, first one and then the other, more like play-acting instead of digging painfully for emotional gold. The thrill comes from play-acting to the meaningful utmost. This kind of story is a great adventure for the writer, and in ratio to his skill and his desire to bring adventure to others, the story succeeds. So go ahead and ham it up. I did, as you will see.

"When he came down into the park, and especially when he neared the place where the light was out, the wooded area known to local teen-agers and their parents as Lovers' Heaven, a ripple ran through the people in the park, a fearful questioning ripple, such as besets a herd of impala when the tiger slips, unseen, among them to single out its victim.

"Miss Cameron was among the first to feel it. She was parked in her little old grey coupe at the edge of the golf course near Lovers' Heaven, backed into the parking place so that she looked across the loop of road into the park proper. It was better than a wide-screen movie. When she tired of watching the shadowy children on the swings and slides, or their parents at the picnic tables, she had only to squint and there in the distance, elevated and lighted to a brilliant promi-nence, was the pool with its diving platform and high white chair for the lifeguard. The chair was empty, but even as Miss Cameron stiffened in indignation, up climbed a bronzed, white-trunked figure.

"The glistening, almost naked teen-agers in their brief, bright suits made a moving frieze against the black sky as they climbed and plummeted and climbed again. Even from this distance Miss Cameron felt the socking rhythm of the juke box. She was conscious of that impudent, lascivious pulse as she turned her head and looked inquiringly toward the miniature golf concession adjoining Lovers' Heaven, off to her left under a canopy of trees hung with yellow insect-repellent lights. There was only one player, a shirt-tail-out boy of twelve or so.

"Turning head and shoulders then, alert as a grizzled old herd cow, Miss Cameron peered into the darkness behind her. She had been parked here for an hour, alone. She hadn't had to spend the evening alone; the girls had wanted her to play bridge at Alma's. But at age forty-four, after evenings and evenings of bridge with the girls, she found it easier, somehow, to be alone. Summers had always been particularly bad, with no papers to grade, not enough money to take a real vacation. But the park had changed all that. Since she had been coming down evenings after supper, Miss Cameron had discovered in herself an enormous capacity for living, though it was at second-hand.

"There was nothing second-hand in the feeling which now came softly and wrapped itself about her throat. It was the most terrible, the most intimate sensation Miss Cameron had ever felt in her life. Intently, wonderingly, forgetting the lighted stage before her, she stared over her shoulder into the darkness."

The stage is set, the Tiger is in the compound and at least one of his potential Victims is alerted, but is Miss Cameron going to be the Victim? And who is the Tiger? By now you probably realize that I had decided to write a whodunit from a new angle. More of a who's-going-to-do-what-to-whom!

The only fair thing, I decided, was to present as completely as possible a cross-section of the people in the park, clearly labeling them potential Tigers and potential Victims. The only way, then, to keep the secret, the suspense necessary for a good story, was to go even farther and have the Tiger unaware that he was the Tiger, as unaware of his own identity as the eventual Victim was of his or her identity.

Actually, this simplified things for me because I didn't have to concern myself with tricking the reader outright, only in the matter of emphasis and accent. I was able to put all my cards on the table and state, flatly, "These are the Tigers and these are the Victims. Now, *you* decide which is going to be the real Tiger and which is going to be his Victim." When the Tiger revealed himself, those readers who had guessed the outcome would be very proud of themselves, and those who hadn't would have been entertained. At least, I hoped so.

One potential Tiger was Woody Bingham who, at the same moment that Miss Cameron stared over her shoulder into the darkness, was standing just inside the dark area which included the real golf course near the closed Pro Shop.

"Woody was seventeen, crew-cropped and burned a shade lighter than chocolate, short, and heavily muscled as a Kodiak bear." He knows Miss Cameron and hates her. She had almost flunked him in English the preceding school year. Woody also has a full head of steam on because his girl, Tanny Archer, has stood him up. "It wasn't the first time she'd stood him up, but this time maybe he'd just try to find out who she'd stood him up for! Head lowered, he stared broodingly toward Lovers' Heaven. Wasn't that a car parked by the concrete slab they sometimes used for dancing? Damn you, Tanny! You, too, Miss Cameron!

"Then, just at the explosion point, he felt it—the creeping, deadly force which held Miss Cameron transfixed, staring into the dark. All of a sudden Woody Bingham wanted to move quickly and silently, his leg muscles corded with the twin efforts of speed and silence. At the same time he was afraid. It was a strange, strong fear; it advised him not to move an inch from where he stood. Not an inch, or he would be lost."

Please note how cleverly this card was laid on the table! At least, I believed so when I was writing it. Is Woody Bingham feeling the Tiger outside himself, or is it perhaps the Tiger within himself?

"At the same moment that Miss Cameron turned her head and Woody Bingham halted in the shadow of the Pro Shop, Susan Hardy, nine years old, small and hardheaded and chubby, was disobeying her mother."

Susan's mother had told her not to go off in the dark by herself, but Susan had done it. She was "way out on the golf course, standing in the darkest dark on the little bridge over the water hazard. At the same moment that Miss Cameron and Woody Bingham were feeling it, Susan felt it. That change in the park's atmosphere. That something like a monstrous, dark, dangerous animal. Somebody was walking over there . . .

closer now. If she moved, it would surely see her and pounce. Cut off from safety, paralyzed, Susan crouched on the little bridge. Underneath it the water lay still and dark as oil."

So now, we have one potential Tiger and two potential Victims. Comes another tiger.

"The lone walker on the golf course was Mr. Murdock. Like Miss Cameron, whom he knew in an offhand fashion, Mr. Murdock was a teacher of English. He taught in the small teachers' college which lay three blocks west of the park."

Mr. Murdock has a more than modest bank account but hasn't taken a vacation in seven years. He teaches summer classes. When the summer term is over it's too hot to go anywhere. Mr. Murdock also suffers terribly from the heat, but never takes off his coat. "Mr. Murdock's coat was an example to the boys, a symbol of respect for the girls. Respect for womanhood, especially young womanhood, was the only subject on which Mr. Murdock was ever articulate outside the classroom." Both classrooms, for Mr. Murdock also teaches a Sunday School class of teen-agers. "The only times he shucked his coat were when he was in the privacy of his home and on those occasions when he went to the gym for a workout with the punching bag. He had been working out at the gym more and more often of late, pummeling the bag with his fists until the salty sweat ran down into his eyes and mouth, sometimes tasting like tears, sometimes like blood. He was on his way to the gym now, wearing his shapeless gray boxing sweatshirt. In his pocket were a key to the gym and his big, old-fashioned flashlight. He was taking his usual short cut through the park."

Mr. Murdock is thirty-nine, a widower. "One afternoon while Mr. Murdock was in his office at the college, in conference with a pert blonde student who needed a B in English, possibly at the exact instant Mr. Murdock reached out, convulsively, and touched a pert round knee, or perhaps at the moment when she leaned forward and whispered, "I'm going to get that B, aren't I, Mr. Murdock?" (She got it, but neither ever looked directly at the other during the remainder of her stay on campus), Mr. Murdock's wife and little girl were killed instantly at the grade crossing south of town, and Mr. Murdock's second-hand yellow convertible smashed beyond repair by the three-thirty express.

Mr. Murdock never bought another automobile; he never smoked another cigarette or held another conference with a student; he never danced after that, and his charming smile was never seen again. Without it, his face became as unmemorable and sexless as a paper plate. He was only thirty-nine, however, and if anyone had taken the trouble to look, he would have seen that Mr. Murdock was in excellent condition for a man who taught English all day. He was in excellent condition, he had the heavy flashlight in his pocket, and he had an active respect for women, especially young girls. He also had the acute powers of observation and imagination possessed by the lonely."

So now we have, in one and the same person, a potential Tiger and a potential Hero.

"In a single glance he saw Susan on the bridge, he correctly identified the faint sheen of headlight glass as a car parked in Lovers' Heaven, and he saw that the street light which should have illumined a portion of that disgraceful spot, was out—burned out or shattered, most likely, by a well-aimed rock.

"Mr. Murdock sucked in his breath and frowned, for he was feeling it, too—that sensation of a tiger on the prowl. Sweating inside the shapeless gray weight of his gym shirt, he put his hand into his pocket. His fingers touched the flashlight, touched and gripped it as he began walking swiftly, quietly, across the dry grass of the fairway. Mr. Murdock, never quite a villain, never quite a hero.

"He came to Susan on the bridge. 'Little girl,' he said in a voice scarcely more than a whisper, at once kind and tortured and infinitely sad, 'you shouldn't be out here in the dark. Can't you see, little girl? The light's burned out.' "

Now enter two potential Heroes. No doubt about them.

"Mr. Murdock wasn't the only one who had noticed the light. At that same moment two policemen in a patrol car were headed for the park. Ab Henry's voice was inflexible, he drove with both hands square on the wheel. 'That damned light—if I had a ladder, I'd get up there and put in a new bulb myself!' Ab had a teen-aged daughter, and it was well known that he broke out in a sweat every time she had a date; the thought of her sitting out there in Lovers' Heaven in a parked car turned Ab white around the mouth. 'If I was your girl, Ab, I wouldn't go near that place,' grinned Harvey. Then he sobered, realizing he had gone too far. 'Look,' said Harvey, ashamed because he didn't have Ab's violent concern for his fellow citizens' welfare, 'When we swing around by the golf course, why not turn the spotlight in under the trees and take a good look?' "

The police are coming. But will they get there in time to stop whatever is going to happen? Well, we'll see. But, first, we have another potential victim.

"Already Elizabeth could hear her mother saying it. *Darling, you're home so early from your lesson. You didn't take the short cut through the park again, after what I said?* No, Mama, Miss Almond let me go before the hour; I came the long way, the safe way. Tonight she would lie about it. Long way, short way, safe way, dangerous way—why can't I choose for myself? Elizabeth thought rebelliously as she stepped onto the path which led under the trees and across the open golf course. I'm nineteen years old, and nothing has ever happened to me. I don't know anything! Oh, she knew how to play the piano, Miss Almond said she had tremendous talent. And last spring in Mr. Murdock's freshman English class, she had taken all the honors. But what about the rest of living? They call this Lovers' Heaven, and there's a car parked over there, Elizabeth thought painfully. I've never been in a parked car with a boy—I've never been anywhere with a boy! Oh, Mama, I wish I were in that parked car with a boy! At that moment Elizabeth stepped on a toad. Both she and the toad gave a soundless shriek.

"She must keep going and get out of this terrible place, for Mama had been right after all. Just help me out of this dark awful place, and I'll wait like Mama says, she promised on an incoherent prayerful note. I'll wait because I'm not ready—I don't know anything about anything— Oh, I'm not ready at all!

"But, ready or not, Elizabeth felt it then. The terrible quickening in the air around her. The force that moved so quietly, so relentlessly. Life, whether she liked it or not, was catching up with Elizabeth Bantting, nineteen years old and never kissed by a boy."

Poor little Victim . . . or is she just a stand-in for the real Victim?

"Tanny Archer had been kissed lots of times, but at that same moment, a few yards away, Tanny began to wish—not that she hadn't stood up Woody Bingham; she still felt no compunction about that—but that she had been a little smarter when Mel turned onto the bumpy dirt lane behind them. It was the only way into Lovers' Heaven, unless you walked across the corner of the golf course. Tonight was her first date with Mel, the first time he had asked her. She didn't usually give a date the first time asked, but she had been waiting for Mel. She had thought, I'm saving Mel for dessert. Or maybe, she figured, he was saving her for dessert. It was funny that after all the waiting, after not feeling a flicker when she stood up Woody, she now felt a kind of panicky longing for him. At least with Woody you knew where you were. With this Mel Harris, 'the nicest boy in town,' she felt uncertain and bewildered. Tanny hated to admit it, even to herself, but she had figured Mel out to be really different. She had expected him to take her some place with lights and music and people to see them. But here they were at the same old stand, and from the way he acted, 'the nicest boy in town' was no different, behind that slow sweet smile, from Woody Bingham! In fact, it was turning out to be a real creepy evening."

It would certainly seem that this Mel could turn out to be a Tiger. Poor Tanny. Beset by Tigers.

"She remembered Woody's bellow over the phone, 'Who're you standing me up for, Tanny—just tell me who!' Was he still mad at her, sitting in his high chair at the pool? After she stood him up, he would have stayed on duty, wouldn't he? Look, you don't belong to Woody Bingham, you don't have to worry. Just the same she had a sudden wish that the trees and the bathhouse weren't in the way; she wished she could see who was on the lifeguard's throne. Heaven was too dark tonight. Off to her right something moved, hurry-hurry, pause, hurry-hurry, pause. In the pauses the quiet seemed to rub against her. Like a big hungry cat, thought Tanny with another shiver. 'This place is creepy.' 'Creepy?' echoed Mel and he, too, seemed to cock an uneasy ear to the evening. Then he laughed. 'You mean creepy like this?' He made spider legs of his fingers; she felt them wiggle up her bare arms; felt him sliding closer. Swiftly Tanny took into account how long she had waited for this date, how it would be if she told him off and had to go back to dating apes like Woody. She came up with a compromise. 'Mel, why not turn on your radio and let's get out on the slab and dance?' Dance with him in the dark—Tanny, you're smart, real smart! But at least the music would break up the creepy, furry quiet.

" 'O.K., Tanny, if you want to dance.' He sounded nice and in the dim glow from the radio he looked nice, with his wavy hair and clean, intent profile. Down at the bottom of Tanny's hard, knowing, calculating little heart something went *zing!* It was like one shy schmaltzy, questioning note from an electric guitar. At first he held her far away and kind of formal. She liked it and didn't like it; but mostly she liked it. Next time he would take her some place where there were people to see them together and say, 'Will you look at that— Tanny Archer with Mel Harris, the nicest boy in town! Maybe we were wrong about Tanny's being so wild. . . .'

"When Mel suddenly stopped dancing and pulled her close and said in an unsteady whisper, 'Aw, Tanny, who wants to dance?' she let him hold her. She let him kiss her and she kissed him back, even as her practical sixth sense warned, *Don't, Tanny, don't. Not here. Not now—*"

Somebody else in the park is worried too.

"Over on the miniature golf course under the hot yellow lights, Jane Conners felt the warning, too. A small, sun-weathered woman in a baggy T-shirt and limp, seersucker shorts, she lifted her cropped head and tested the warning ripple on the stale August air. She tested and did not like what her sixth sense told her. She called to the scuffling knot of children at the fifth hole. Her own were there and three neighbor kids. Bringing the neighbor kids had been a diplomatic gesture, since the Conners were new in town. 'Aw, Ma, we didn't finish yet. We gotta finish this game, Ma!'

" 'Get in there!' She gave the oldest and loudest a swat for good measure because when Jane Conners made up her mind it was made up. It was a shame to cut the kids short, but something screwy was fixing to happen in this park, and if she had learned anything, it was not to be around when something screwy happened. Take Deke, he was just the other way. Deke?

"She stiffened. Her eyes darted here, there, and yonder. Just a minute ago he had been right over there on that bench, drinking out of a paper cup. She had figured it was water or Coke—they didn't allow beer in this park. But wasn't there a place that sold beer right across the highway? 'Where's your daddy?' she asked sharply. 'Any of you see which way he walked off?' They hadn't seen Deke walk off—didn't care about Deke; all they cared about was finishing the game. But roughly, with swats and slaps, she pushed them into the station wagon. 'Now don't a one of you get out of there,' she said fiercely. 'I'm going over to the swimming pool and get your daddy.' As she crossed the road, her eyes darted, searching for the big shape, slack around the middle but still powerful, the up-flung curly head. If he had turned to acting, Deke could have been a movie star, he was that good-looking. Did he

watch the young girls in their snips of bathing suits because he couldn't help it, or was it just to tease her? He
doesn't really care about them, she told herself stoutly,
or else he wouldn't still be with her. She rounded the
bathhouse. Deke wasn't at the pool.

"As she hurried back to the station wagon, behind
her the juke box thumped and wailed, heightening her
intuition that something strange and bad was about to
happen. Wildly she glanced up and down the winding
park road. Far away at the entrance she saw the police
car turn in. Deke! Deke! In a fierce ecstasy of love, she
willed him to her as she had done countless times in
the past. But he didn't come. Jane Conners felt the
weight of all the years of pretense and conniving. The
years of talking for Deke and thinking for him and
watching him in ways that wouldn't look like watching.
The years of explaining Deke to the neighbors, to his
bosses, even to his own kids. 'Daddy was just kidding
around when he hurt your arm, Arliss. . . . Daddy
thought it was just your old worn-out doll, Loretta,
when he threw it in the trash.' Years of explaining and
moving on to another town and finding Deke another
job in another service garage. No trouble there because, in his head, Deke had the natural know-how to
take a car apart and put it back together. The trouble
was the other things Deke had in his head.

"Standing there in the road, Jane Conners prayed.
'God, if you just see he doesn't get in trouble this time,
I'll do it. I'll take him to one of those doctors and whatever the doc says—if Deke's got to be sent away and
shut up in one of those places—I'll even do that. If you

just keep him out of trouble this time . . . help me find him.' "

Another Tiger. The most likely Tiger yet. *Saved, you will notice, for the last on the list.* Two clear-cut Tigers now, Woody Bingham and Deke; two slightly complicated Tiger-or-Hero types, Mr. Murdock and Mel, "the nicest boy in town." Four Victims: Miss Cameron, Susan Hardy, Elizabeth, and Tanny Archer; plus two definite Heroes, the police coming with their spotlight. Just for good measure, shouldn't we have another hero?

"Charles Lattimore could have told her (Jane Conners) which way the big man had gone. Charles was twelve and he noticed lots of things. He could have told anyone who would listen that the thermometer on the back of the miniature golf stand registered eighty-two degrees, that it was impossible to make the seventh hole in one stroke, that one of the kids in the station wagon had stolen a ball, a green one, and that the big curly-haired man on the bench had been drinking beer out of a paper cup before he got up and walked away. Charles knew by the smell. Charles was not ever going to drink beer or smoke cigarettes, or use tobacco in any form. As soon as they would take him, he was going to join the F.B.I. Throughout the long hot summer, Charles had engaged in a rigorous physical fitness program. Only one soft drink a day and every day, without fail, some kind of physical exercise. So here he was. It was only nine by his waterproof, shockproof wrist watch, and he didn't have to be home until nine-thirty. But all of a sudden, when he saw he was the only player left on the course, Charles decided to start home. There's something funny going on around here, thought Charles, his skin prickling. He saw the police car turning in at the park entrance. He considered stopping the car and asking for a ride home. He could tell them his mother worried and he should've been home an hour ago, but he'd tripped on a tree root and sprained his ankle and couldn't walk well. . . . This unworthy flash of deceit and chicken-heartedness was so swiftly gone that Charles could very well say he'd never had it. He would walk home, of course.

"Turning, he stared resolutely into the gloom of Lovers' Heaven. Anybody in there would be too busy kissing to bother him! He was starting to go and turn in his ball and club at the stand when, simultaneously, the prickling of his skin grew worse, and he realized that the light at the edge of the real golf course, the light he had counted on, was out. At the moment, the golf club in Charles' hand ceased abruptly to be a golf club, the property of someone else. It became, in the simplest and most natural fashion, a weapon. His own weapon. Because if something was in there among the dark trees, a big mean boxer or—(or what, Charles? What is it that makes your skin crawl?)—not even Sherlock Holmes would go in there empty-handed. Without thinking any more about it, Charles stepped quietly off the miniature golf course onto the trackless moor.

"So it was that at one and the same time Charles stole a golf club, Jane Conners made a long overdue promise, Susan Hardy wished she had minded her mother, Elizabeth discovered that life could be a squashy toad, Tanny lost her practicality, and Miss Cameron—well, Miss Cameron was the first to recognize that soft black ripple across the park for what it actually was. Miss Cameron was the first to understand when the ripple took on form and purpose, and the outcome became inevitable. The tiger had selected its victim.

"With the soft darkness wrapping tight about her sagging throat, remembering the deadly evenings of bridge with the girls, the rubber plants and handkerchiefs for Christmas, the slow drip-drip of the kitchen faucet in her little apartment, Miss Cameron felt a surge of terrible joy. But it isn't you, Miss Cameron. Not you. Not yet. Not in this fashion.

"Tanny's scream split the summer night like a sharp, silver knife."

So now we know the Victim. But who is the Tiger? And, who will be the Hero?

"Something had told her (Tanny) to stop kissing and run. But before she could, a light stabbed her face. In the darker darkness which followed, she heard the crunch of metal on bone and flesh, a soft heavy thud on the concrete slab. Run now, Tanny! Crazy—whoever it is—panting—sobbing—whispering—crazy! But Mel was hurt. Wasn't it Mel who had fallen—?

"Hands found her then, strong fumbling hands which caressed and then tightened convulsively on her throat. Through the roaring in her ears, she heard a sobbing whisper—'Kiss me—please kiss me—' Then suddenly the hands flew wide, leaving her throat free. Above the sounds of fearful struggle at her feet, Tanny screamed.

"The police car spotlight slammed into the darkness. It glanced off Miss Cameron's spotless windshield. It caught Susan Hardy running like a fat little chipmunk to her mother. It paused on Elizabeth's white, sickened face; then, hurrying, it swept past the struggle under the trees and found Charles crouching, his golf club up-raised but unused. Charles had just made a startling discovery; in the dark it is almost impossible to tell tiger from victim, unless you happen to be one or the other.

"At last, in a hasty double take, the spotlight swept back to the scene under the trees, to Tanny standing and Mel rising from a still, silent shape on the concrete. In the sudden glare Tanny and Mel were looking at each other in wonder.

"Tanny had been kissed, whistled at, ogled, fought over and whispered about. But never before had she been defended and saved from violent attack; she had no illusions about that, having felt the hands at her throat and the mad whisper on her cheek. Tanny was a very knowing and practical girl, even a little hard at times. But now as she stared at her rescuer's face— the terrible, quivering, boy-into-man face with blood seeping down from the split scalp—her heart went *zing* with uncompromising finality. As for Mel, he had kissed a lot of girls lately, trying to live down that 'nicest boy in town' title he'd somehow gotten stuck with. He had intended to complete his metamorphosis at Tanny's expense. Instead, he had defended her, shed blood for her, maybe even killed for her. Suddenly all doubts about his manhood were gone. And, with them, all confusion as to Tanny's place in his life. *This is my girl.*

"So engrossed were they in these mutual discoveries, they forgot the still, quiet bulk at their feet. Old Ab and his rookie were already running to them across the golf course before Tanny looked down and cried in a clear, carrying young voice, 'Why, it's Mr. Murdock!' And then, staring at the shocked, incredulous expression which contorted that familiar-unfamiliar face even in unconsciousness, she whispered, 'Poor Mr. Murdock. . . .'

"And so it was, Mr. Murdock in his shapeless gray sweatshirt with his cracked flashlight lying to one side. Poor Mr. Murdock. For after all is said and done, who is the tiger but the victim? What is darkness but a light gone out?"

In all immodesty, I must confess that I love those last two lines! And there in my confession lies the joy of writing an Out-of-Nowhere Story. Freed from the coils of self as recognized by self, the old day-by-day you, your day-by-day experiences and emotions shoved aside, you pull out all the stops and have yourself an adventure!

The measure of your own enjoyment in this adventure is, I think, the eventual measure of your readers' enjoyment. So go ahead and play it big! I am convinced that the author's *exuberance* is actually what puts over the Out-of-Nowhere Story. This one, for instance, has entirely too many characters for a short story (count 'em!), but sheer exuberance and delight in the adventure prevented my letting any one of them get out of hand or get off the roller-coaster story track. Each was a story in himself, but I caught them, impaled all of them on the same pinpoint of truth (Who am I—Tiger, Victim, Hero?) and held them there until each of them knew who he was. At least, that's what I intended.

Go now and listen to your own voices from out-of-nowhere!

Six

BASIC STORY PATTERNS

PERSONAL Experience, Personal Emotion, and The Out-of-Nowhere Story. Though considerably different in content and development, they have in common the fact that I was possessed and obsessed by each of them in idea form and during the actual writing.

I also knew exactly where I was going with each before I began the actual composition. I can't overemphasize the importance of knowing exactly where you're going before you begin, actually, to write your story. I have heard of writers who sat down and wrote whatever came into their heads, then took such material and made stories of it. That is all very well and good, but in the initial writing these writers were *not* engaged in the actual composition of a story. What they were doing is, in essence, the same thing which I hoped to accomplish for you—less laboriously, less wastefully, more excitingly, more effectively, with the self-starter exercises in Chapter Two: stirring up story ideas.

The point I am trying to make is that when you sit down to *write* a story, to save time, lessen the agony, and enhance the pleasure, you must *already* have your idea and must have allowed it to come to sprouting age. You must know *exactly* where you are going, *exactly* what you intend to accomplish. You must know how you're going to get *out* of your story, or else it is not the time for you to get *in*. You have cheated and cut short your germination period, which is bad for your story and will ultimately be worse, because editors are not in the habit of buying stories which do not provide inevitable, satisfying endings for a substantial portion of their magazine's readers.

Just because the ending of a story is normally read last does not mean that the ending is less important than the barbed and well-aimed hook in the beginning. If you hook your reader and then fall on your face, dragging the reader down with you, no one is going to forgive you, least of all yourself, especially when the editors keep firing your stories back to you as fast as you send them out!

To fail to bring your story to a definite conclusion, to fail to end it satisfactorily, is like packing your beautiful idea into half a capsule. The whole thing spills and dribbles away to a meaningless nothing.

What is this capsule called plot, anyway?

It's the difference between a beautiful story idea, as wild and free-wheeling as the wind, as sweet and unmanageable as springtime, as powerful as lightning and just as impossible to catch hold of and hold onto— the difference between that and a marketable product.

The plot is nothing in itself, but you can't capture or

make meaningful the good idea without it. You can't successfully market it, either! The bigger and more powerful the idea, the stouter and stronger the plot you must use to contain it. Happily enough, if you know when you start writing exactly where you're going, the plot will form almost of itself. By knowing where you're going, I mean where your hero, your main characters, are going. And you can know where they are going only in direct ratio to how well you, the writer, are acquainted with them. Know your heroes well. Even for a short-short story, you must know the people you're writing about better than you know yourself.

If you have been thinking of a short story as a sort of trick and yourself as a magician successfully performing this trick, stop thinking that way. *A short story is not a trick. It is people, real people caught in a moment of truth, exaggerated, perhaps, but still truth.*

All fundamental truths have been with us since time began; the same goes for plots. They have all been acted out many, many times in real life. *But not as you see them.* There is your selling point. *You.* The truth as *you* see it, acted out by people as *you* see them acting it.

Never forget what you're selling—not plot, certainly not tricks which can be learned by rote and practice; but truth as you see it, packaged as you alone can package it.

Now that you have aroused your subconscious, found your idea, allowed it to germinate, become familiar with the people who will embody it in your small approximation of life—now that you have arrived at the point of knowing exactly where you want to go and what you wish to accomplish, we will talk about the practical aspects of packaging.

What *about* this tangible package—this capsule, this plot? Of necessity, it must be something tangible that you, as well as the editors and, you sincerely hope, your eventual readers, can catch hold of and hang onto when the going gets rough.

Here, in the simplest terms that I have been able to evolve, is your plot, your package—the makings of it, at least. There are any number of formulas going. You hear of new ones all the time, but they all boil down to the same thing.

You can say that a story is composed of two parts, six parts, four parts—but I'll say three parts.

In the first part of the story, your hero's problem or dilemma is stated immediately. Universal problems, hard problems, are always best. Any time you put your hero in a flimsy box it goes without saying that you will end up with a flimsy story.

Along with the presentation of your hero's problem, you present your hero, as entertainingly, as strikingly, as touchingly, as fully and as briefly, as possible. You say to your reader, "Here is someone I think you should know." And then you make him glad for the introduction, if for no other reason than that he has never met a person *exactly* like this before in his life. I say *exactly* because everybody has already met lots of somebodies *almost* like everybody else he knows.

Present your hero to the reader in such a way that the reader cannot help caring about the hero's success or failure, whichever is inevitable.

In this first section of your story there is also the skillful planting of something which will, in the end, provide or expedite the solution to your hero's problem and the conclusion of your story. In most writer-teacher circles, this thing is known as the "gimmick." It's a distasteful little word that smacks of commercialism, so let's call it the Artful Device and think of it as the writer's truest friend.

The Artful Device may be anything, literally anything under the sun, even the sun itself. A pair of red shoes, a certain fragrance, a handkerchief, a doll buggy, a hair ribbon, a time of day, a storm, a pocketknife, a gesture, a song, a piece of lead pipe, the odor of moth balls, the taste of hard candy, the sound of china breaking. The list is almost inexhaustible.

The skillful use of this device is imperative for a good story, especially for a beginning writer. Notice that I did say "skillful." A clumsily used Artful Device is worse than none at all. It must be as integrated with the story it serves as the ankle bone is with the leg bone. It must be as unobtrusive in the beginning as your hero's own shadow. For the climax, it must be as explosive as the charge of dynamite needed to burst the hero from his box. Explosive, that is, for the hero.

The Artful Device or gimmick, if properly used, is a two-sided thing. The first several times, the innocent, artless face is shown. At the high dramatic point of your story, turn your device quickly, and there is the terrible, wonderful, all-knowing face of truth confronting your hero!

As an example: Your heroine is a woman just past her youthful freshness, but by no means faded yet. She has never married. She has had several proposals, but, following her mother's advice, she is still waiting for the right man, forceful and successful, for whom she can safely give up her well-paying job to keep the beautiful home which he will provide; for whom she will perform all the functions inherent in being the wife of a forceful, successful man. Her immediate problem is how to get rid of her current beau, a sweet fellow who is very much in love with her, who persists in proposing again and again, but who is not anybody's idea of a forceful, successful man. She likes him very much, enjoys his company and wishes above all else to avoid hurting him any more than necessary, but she must discourage him, once and for all. She wants no repetition of the first time she turned down a proposal, years ago, on the advice of her mother who maintained that a persistent but hopeless suitor, if allowed out of kindness to hang around, would discourage and keep away the eligible, who might misinterpret his constant presence. And her mother had been right, oh, so right! Lettie acknowledged this and understood the rightness even more now that she was older; she held nothing against her mother.

The trouble was that when she had told the boy she wouldn't marry him, he had gone roaring off into the night in his borrowed automobile, and crashed into a bridge abutment and was killed. Even now, thirteen years later, she cannot remember it without curling inside like a tight, anguished fist. But her mother had been right, so right. If she had married the boy, all the sweetness would have been wrung out of it by now, and she would not even have the memory of that sweetness, because he was the kind, like Don now, who would never have amounted to much. Oh, he had been sweet, so very sweet. Unable to buy her orchids, he had bought her violets, or more likely he had picked them himself, wild violets from the wooded area behind his mother's house.

"But even then you wanted orchids, my dear," her mother had reminded her, time and time again. "It's not your fault; there's no harm in wanting orchids. Never settle for less than the best." And it is true; she still wants orchids. Don will never be able to buy them for her. So, tonight she must break it off, clean and neat and final but with kindness, because Don, in spite of his lack of forcefulness, his helplessness in the business world, is really a fine sweet person. Older, too, and more level-headed, so there cannot possibly be another tragedy like the first. She shivers, even now, thirteen years later, remembering it.

And there you have it—problem stated, heroine established, and The Artful Device placed on the table, showing one face but keeping the other face hidden. (The above is *not* dramatized! Why don't you stop and try to put all this information into story—say, three catchy, dramatic, forward-moving pages of *story?*)

The second part of a story, as I see it, is the hero or heroine acting on the problem and the problem acting on the hero or heroine. There are set-backs and go-forwards. In the story I have used as an example, Lettie has her date with Don, torn with the necessity of refusing him, of making it final, but in the kindest, gentlest way. Several times during the evening she takes a stab at telling him that this is their last date, but each time she is unable to go through with it. At last, however, as they are walking out of the theater (to which Don has insisted on taking her, though she knows he can't afford it), she at last is propelled to such a peak of exasperation that she is ready to tell him.

Imagine that ever since the beginning of the story you have been building a wave curling upward, upward. We are now at a point just before the peak of the wave, the climax, the decision point, whatever you wish to call it. The Artful Device is waiting to perform its planned function. Lettie is completely exasperated when Don stops beside a little old lady selling bunches of field violets, and with what Lettie knows to be his very last dime, buys a bunch and presents them to her with some nonsensical compliment, such as the fact that they match her eyes. Nobody's eyes are that color!

Now we enter the third part of the story. We are poised on that spot just before the heroine's decision point, the peak of the wave from which she must choose to slide here or there. Don is handing her the violets with a compliment and a new proposal of marriage. *Now,* now, when she is so exasperated is the time to tell him!

(At this point, if it were not for your Artful Device, the story would lack sharpness and focus, two things a successful short story should have.)

As Lettie is forced to accept the violets, as she opens her mouth to refuse both them and their donor, once and for all, she feels the thin tender stems between her fingers, and the faint fragrance rises. Suddenly she is back in that other time thirteen years ago, accepting violets from Joe. In that instant Joe and Don and Time are fused to create an explosive charge. Suddenly Lettie knows that, had it not been for her mother, she would have married Joe. Violets would have been enough; she wouldn't have wanted orchids. Her mother had wanted orchids for her. She knows this, at last, looking into Don's face which is also Joe's face. The reason for Don is Joe, and the fact that she had truly loved Joe. Loved him enough, had it not been for her mother, to be happy with violets instead of orchids. Joe is dead. But Don isn't. She loves him. She has a second chance.

But has she the courage to take it? Thirteen years older, set in her ways, an orchid appetite well developed through the years? The first time with Joe it would have been all right, but now how can it possibly be right? Then, with the smell of the violets stinging her nostrils, with tears in her eyes for herself, for Joe and for Don, she tells Don she will marry him.

In other words, the feel and scent of the violets has blown a hole through the impassable brambles of Lettie's conditioned reflexes, but at the moment all is darkness down there at the end of the passage to the future. She is faint and weak at the thing she has done.

Now is the time for your heroine's reward or punishment, whichever is appropriate, inevitable, and satisfying to you personally, and whichever you think will seem appropriate, inevitable, and satisfying to your readers.

For this particular story, I think Don would say something indicating that Lettie would be free to continue in her career-job, something to show that he, perhaps, understands her better than she does herself; that he understands her need to continue her career, the one thing at which she has been successful—that he loves her in spite of this knowledge, which is more than all the forceful, successful men had done. They had actually resented her success. But with Don she is free to be the self that time and circumstance have made her, and at the same time, she can enjoy love.

The format of the story is this: Part One—state problem, establish hero, plant the ultimate solution along with The Artful Device. Part Two—hero acts on problem; problem acts on hero. Set-backs and go-forwards. Just before decision point, bring out Device. Third Part—decision made. Dark side of Device still turned to hero. Then suddenly there is the bright side, if it is a reward story. If it is a punishment story, the dark side continues to face the hero. Or else the bright side turns and the hero sees it, but it is out of reach and gone from him forever.

When you have written so many stories you can't remember them all, you will find that it isn't necessary to actually write *all* the parts of this basic story pattern. You may write stories which end (on paper) a split second after the decision point, for instance. But only a very skillful writer can set up a story so perfectly, so vividly and dramatically, that it finishes writing itself in the reader's imagination.

You may write stories in which the second part of the story is omitted completely, or compressed into a single sentence. But, again, this variation takes a highly skilled artist. You may write stories in which The Artful Device or Gimmick is so subtly buried in the story and integrated with it that it is scarcely recognizable as such. You may write stories in which reward and punishment are one and the same. More power to you—but remember that this takes skill, which comes, almost invariably, from writing, writing, writing. So let's go now and write, write, write!

Seven

A GRAB BAG OF DO'S AND DON'TS

You are finally ready to package your story idea, actually to write it. Here are some tips which I hope you will find helpful in this writing:

Viewpoint isn't quite the ornery beast it's made out to be. *Viewpoint is simply where you, the writer, are while telling your story.* You may be (1) inside your hero, (2) inside an observer-narrator (which is always less forceful, but some stories require it); (3) inside your villain (which isn't as odd a way to tell your hero's story as you may imagine; think about it!); (4) inside one character and then another and then another (multiple viewpoint was used, of necessity, in my Out-of-Nowhere story. It's wonderful fun but only if your story requires it!); or (5) with God in his Heaven, looking down. (This viewpoint requires an immensely powerful story, however. For most stories it is the least compelling viewpoint of all—probably because, while most of us can identify with hero or villain, none of us can identify with God. This omniscient viewpoint can be used—sparingly and only when necessary—as can the closely-akin observer-narrator viewpoint, for story openings or endings; to survey the scene before moving into your hero's viewpoint, and/or to sum up in the last paragraph. But do be careful!)

There is one other viewpoint I didn't mention because it's so awful: You, the writer, are sitting in the air, plainly visible, at some point about two feet away from your hero's left shoulder. He goes through the motions of the story, and *you* sit there and tell us when he's sad and when he's happy, and why he did this and why he did that. *You* tell us he hates his father, but we don't believe it for a minute, and if we do, we don't give a hang; the hero is just a robot, and who gives a hang whether a robot hates his father or not? We strongly suspect he doesn't have a father. *You* are his parent, the very worst kind of parent who doesn't trust his or her offspring to speak for himself. What's even more maddening and stultifying, you speak for every member of your little story family! You do it all, and it gets pretty darn tiresome. Nobody but a moronic reader is going to put up with it for a minute—and readers aren't morons.

Beginning writers are most often guilty of using this viewpoint. Don't you be guilty of it. Pick somebody— the hero, the villain, I don't care, *somebody*—to get inside of. And I do mean inside—right there under the skin and through the bone down to the fingertips; into the heart and eyes and nerve centers; in the ears and nose—and *stay there*. Don't you dare see anything or smell anything or feel anything or need anything or love anything or hate anything that your host can't see, hear, touch, smell, feel, need, love, or hate! Don't you dare.

And that's viewpoint. . . .

*   *   *

Don't be a slow starter. Get off the ground in a hurry.

Don't withhold vital information or create false suspense. Give your reader a fair chance. Put all or as many of your cards on the table as you can afford to. The only person or persons you withhold information from are your hero and/or the other characters in your story. *True suspense comes from showing your reader all the cards.* Then both of you, writer and reader, can settle down to watch what happens to your *hero* or main character, who can see only one of the cards. Your story *is* what the hero does with this incomplete information. Which road will he take?

Don't hang around after the story is over. If you have set the story up properly and played it out at the right pace, if you have been fair with the reader, there will be no necessity for hanging around to explain what happened, or to justify it. And when your story is finished, don't trespass on the future. Leave that to your reader's imagination. After all, his imagination is probably just as original as yours, and just as satisfying to him.

Don't force your personal philosophy of life onto your poor reader in bucket loads. Give it to him in spoonfuls of chocolate syrup. Make it obvious in your plot and characters. *Show,* always *show,* instead of stating, telling, sermonizing, preaching. If you have a message, don't preach it to the reader; *show* it in the action and unfolding of your story and in the changing and development of your characters.

Use as few characters as possible for the purposes of unfolding your story.

Don't look down on your reader. Nothing is meaner or will get you fewer readers. Nobody, absolutely nobody, likes to be patted on the head in a patronizing way—not even dogs!

Don't force yourself to write the same plots or ideas that are being printed in the magazines. The editors have already bought those. This doesn't necessarily mean they want to keep buying similar stories. Use your own ideas and if you discover, as you always will, that your plot, your capsule, isn't unique, just remember that no plot is unique. Your own uniqueness brought to bear on this old-as-the-hills thing is what you're selling—your own viewpoint on life—yourself.

Don't go in for big, grand, vague generalities. Be specific. Don't, for instance, attempt to write a story on the broad assumption that Good is better than Evil. Everybody knows that! Narrow it down to a single specific Good in the person of some memorable hero and pit him against an opposing specific Evil embodied in an equally interesting villain. Better still, embody Good and Evil in a single human being!

Avoid writing about places you haven't been or situations in life that you know absolutely nothing about. The trick here is to transpose to what you know. For instance, you think of a story involving a girl with a billion dollars and a beachcomber without a nickel. But you don't know a girl with a billion dollars or a

genuine beachcomber. What do you do? You make
the girl the richest girl in your own hometown. You
make the boy a kid who can't keep a job even at the
filling station, a boy who really doesn't want a job.
That story you can write.

You think of a story involving voodoo. You simply
must write a story about voodoo. O.K. But make it
local hometown voodoo: A local club woman gets hold
of an old book on the subject and decides to use it to
become president of the garden club or something. She
works voodoo on her rival with hilarious success or
touching failure. *That* you may write to your great
profit and pleasure, but any attempt to write seriously
of voodoo in its own locale, completely unknown to
you, would most likely result in no pleasure or profit
to anyone, least of all, you.

One of the commonest and most depressing comments that editors make when rejecting stories, especially a beginner's story, is that nasty word "contrived."
The best way to avoid getting that particular comment
is to make certain before you begin to write, while your
idea is still germinating or while you are formulating
your plot, that every action of your hero is well and
soundly motivated, grounded in your hero's truth and
not in flimsy haphazard fiction.

Never, under any circumstances, force your hero to
do something simply to fit your plot. The plot must fit
the hero like a nylon stretchy sock, and the hero be
born out of your original burning story idea. Each
thing in your story must complement every other thing.
If so, your characters' actions will spring naturally
from true motivations and, incidentally, you will have

no kickback from editors about that old bugaboo "coincidence." You won't get comments saying, "This story is too pat"—which is also one of the more maddening comments, making you wish to do nothing less than go to New York and pat the offending editor over the head with a meat cleaver! But don't do it. The editor is probably right in his evaluation.

In the interest of good sound motivation, keep your plot simple and to the point. If you try to write a story too full of turns and twistings and physical mechanics, it'll be like cooking a twenty-course meal. Watch the peas . . . watch the roast . . . make the salad . . . blanch the almonds . . . stir the soup . . . get it all done and serve it at exactly the right temperature at the proper time. You'll be run ragged, you'll wish you'd never started, and more than likely you'll burn half the courses, and nobody will have a good time at your dinner party.

A simple, well-prepared family meal is your best bet. Everything will be brought to the table just at the proper peak of heat and cold, crispness and color and flavor, because you had time and energy to do more than fly frantically from refrigerator to stove to sink; you had time to put more into the meal than its mere physical preparation: You put your love into it and made it a great gift.

The simple story is the easiest and the most rewarding to bring to perfection. As an example, I'd like to mention my story, "Precious Moment," in the May, 1961, *McCall's*. My hero's problem was this, no less, no more: by what name should he call his mother-in-law, who happened to be staying in his home? How this problem was eventually solved was the story. Too slim? Well, maybe so, but *McCall's* bought it. I think the reason they bought it was that my hero, being the person he was, was honestly and truly bound up in his dilemma, obsessed with his problem. He was a nice man, and he just had to find some form of address other than "you" to express his very real gratitude, his liking for this woman who was his wife's mother.

Find your stories in your daily life and in the lives around you. Don't attempt to be too much out of this world. Don't strain for novel effects, or strange and wonderful philosophies to the detriment of your story, at the risk of completely losing your poor reader.

Don't strive and contrive to be different. You are already slightly different from the rest of humanity; you don't have to strain for it. Your true readable uniqueness is to be found in what you see in your own back yard; how you feel walking into your kitchen on a sunny morning; how you feel about your children, your husband or wife. But you're not so different from the rest of humanity that you stick out like a sore thumb. Don't strive to make yourself seem different. Who likes "sore-thumb" stories?

Don't be afraid to use people you know as characters. Unless you use them just as they are, including physical peculiarities and circumstances, the real people will never recognize themselves.

The nature of your hero's problem determines whether you should state it bluntly or subtly in the opening part of your story. If, for instance, your hero's problem is a deep-seated fear that he was lacking in manliness, the statement of the problem would, of necessity, have to be subtle. On the other hand, if your hero's problem is the fact that his new home is being condemned to allow a new turnpike to be built, then the problem could be stated as clearly and bluntly as possible.

Among your considerations as to the manner in which to state your hero's problem is the matter of whether your hero recognizes his own problem as such. Sometimes your hero recognizes only some corner or portion of his own problem in the beginning of your story. In that case, it's up to you to give the reader the whole problem, in some manner. The hero may not recognize his own problem completely, but the reader *must* recognize it.

Give your hero the devil, harry him, worry him, shred him into little pieces, if you must, but always make what happens to him seem inevitable, *and always be good to your reader.*

If you must knock your reader down, pick him up immediately afterward.

Don't annoy your reader, for instance, by giving an unsympathetic hero everything on a platter, or giving your good sympathetic hero a kick.

Concerning the matter of sympathy, I think every story needs one character whom the reader can get right in there and holler for. Ever so often I forget this vital fact. It is one of the few disadvantages I have found in having written for so many years, so prolific-ally: I find it hard to realize that the average reader (if there is such an animal!) does not share my very necessary and highly developed obsession with people, sympathetic or not. Even the exotic story should have someone in it with whom Average Reader can sympathize, for whom he can cheer. A sympathetic character is mandatory for the simple story. By simple story, I don't mean a weak story or a slight story or a trite story. Nothing in this world that's worth writing about is trite to the person to whom it is happening. And the person to whom it is happening is your reader—through the medium of your hero. Remember that. It is your business to write stories which have happened a million times, which are still happening by the thousands, and which will probably go on happening, repeating themselves over and over to the end of time —it is your impossible task to write these same stories without triteness.

Here is a short incomplete list of often-repeated stories:

> Man against nature
> Man against himself
> Man against man
> Man against God
> Young love story
> Housewife story
> Middle-aged love story
> Small boy and grandma or grandpa
> Career girl story
> Ambition story
> Young married story
> Young parents story
> First baby story
> Last baby story

Unexpected baby story
Everyday adventure
Exotic adventure

And so on . . . you can make your own list.

You must write these same old stories in such a way that they are not trite, in such a way that they have the cry of the human heart in them instead of simply your own crying need for money. . . . Recognize before you plunge into this business of writing that it is really a sort of calling; in many ways like being called to the ministry or the medical profession. Recognize that, like doctors and ministers, we writers must formulate some conclusions about the human race and feel some compassion for people before we can successfully write of even one invented, created, imagined member of it in this thing called a short story.

By the same token, and because writing is the most intimate business in the world, a writer should go a step further and formulate some conclusions and feel some compassion for himself. He's a member of the human race, isn't he? And right on hand at all times— the most available specimen. If you study the human race, and yourself, you'll discover all sorts of story springboards.

If there is to be any triteness in your story, by all means let it be in the plot, the vehicle, never, under any circumstances, in your hero, your people, and their emotions. The basic emotions, however simple and time-worn, are almost invariably powerful and universally absorbing. Therefore, don't sell short the emotional pattern, the emotional force of your story, for fear of triteness. If you are truly moved by a story idea, you can't be trite if you try!

It is not enough to write a merely competent story to sell on today's market; you must give it *more,* that intangible something which only you can give by feeling deeply and honestly, and writing, always, with all the skill at your command. If you have the skill, be subtle in the writing of your story, but never obscure. Subtlety is a delight to the trained reader, but obscurity is maddening to anyone. *Deliberate obscurity on the part of the author is unforgivable.*

The best cure I know for inadvertent obscurity is to put the story aside after completing the first draft. Forget it; let it cool for several days or weeks, depending on how swiftly you make the transition from the author of the greatest story ever written to the cold-eyed judge of the same story. After this cooling period, read the story as a judge, not as the proud author, and more than likely the obscurities will become apparent to you. You can do something about them while the story still belongs to you, before it becomes the concern of the magazine editorial staffs.

Don't be coy, cute, or arch. These are harsh words to have thrown at you by an editor! I know.

Don't generalize, especially in a short story. Be specific within generalities. Have something very specific and very definite to say, but don't *say* it. Remember that you're not writing an essay, a sketch, a treatise, or a sermon. You're writing a story. Don't *say,* don't *tell—show.* Make your reader taste, touch, smell, think, as well as see, and if you have illustrated your message properly, he will get it. He will get it, and he will have been entertained at the same time.

Entertainment is what your reader thinks he wants. Entertainment is what your reader is buying and what the editors attempt to buy for your reader. Make your reader laugh and make him cry, or make him do both at the same time, and he will take your message to heart, painlessly, without, in many instances, ever knowing that you intended a message. This is just as well, because most readers have a built-in resistance to messages and bits of advice from others.

Don't stand on your mountain peak and look down from your lofty height and tell your reader how best to live his life! *Show* him how to live it, and he will never know you *told* him, and he will love you forever instead of resenting you. Be human with your reader. Write your story as you really feel it. Be natural and easy. Make all your characters as natural in their separate identities as possible.

It also helps to give each of your characters, however noble, some relatively harmless faults. As far as I know, all of the great and beloved characters of fiction have had at least one human fault. The reason for this, I'm sure, is that absolute goodness cannot be embodied in any human being without incurring reader resentment and/or boredom.

Beguile and enchant the reader with all the forces at your command. Don't be shy. Go on and tell your story with all its hurting, joyful force. Your reader won't mind; he'll love it. Your reader isn't as afraid of honest human emotion as you may think he is.

Don't take excursions, little unnecessary side trips,

before you can bring yourself to come to grips with the big scenes. Get right in there with your characters. Only by so doing will you become powerful enough to lift your readers out of their ruts to the necessary level of perception, sympathy, and involvement.

Don't renege on your story. Don't walk around it. Don't ramble, don't amble, but don't go so fast that your reader can't keep up with you. Pace is another of those things which cannot be evaluated when you're too close to your story, but which become apparent after the cold-storage treatment recommended earlier.

At all times while writing your story, be aware that a short story is a very small package; therefore, you have no time or words to waste, no room for mistakes or side-shows.

Tone is very important. Is your story going to be one which bubbles as unrestrainedly as champagne, or is it going to be like slow gentle rain tapping at the windows on a cool autumn evening? Or as artless as a bouquet of field flowers gathered in the early morning? Is it going to be as forthright and honest as butter-milk, or as romantic as an orchid, as touchingly stately as an old, old judge in his robes, or is it going to enter your reader's life like a puppy chasing a yellow butter-fly?

This is what I call "tone." Decide before you begin writing, or at least before you complete the first page, the tone which best suits your story. Decide on the tone and stay with it unless, of course, your story by its very nature is a study in tones, or you feel that your story must be sharply contrasting in tone to achieve the nec-essary and desired effect. But stories which require this treatment don't come up too often. Usually, it is best to stick to a single tone.

Above all, be human. Remember, most parents love their children but can't help being annoyed by them at times; most husbands and wives love each other, but can't help getting annoyed with each other at times; most teen-agers like their parents but can't help getting annoyed with them at times.

Be careful in the use of symbols. Symbols are tricky. Don't overload your story with them. One good one is usually enough for a story, and that one must be an integral part of the story. For instance, an old-fashioned iron fence might be used as a symbol of snobbery in the mind of a newsboy who falls in love with the princess who lives behind the fence in the big house. In the end the newsboy must either tear down the fence, literally, or come to see it, to understand it for what it actually is—a last pathetic bulwark between pride and the world.

Be *very* careful in the matter of making your characters symbols. A symbol is much weaker and much less lovable than a genuine, unique human being.

Go now, and write your story. Write it lean and human, with compassion, with craft and care and great love for humanity and for the story. At the moment of writing, it is your *only* story. Each story as you write it should be your only story. This is simply another way of saying, live today to its fullest and richest and best, for tomorrow you may not be around—but, most likely, you will be. Most likely you will write many, many stories, each better than the last.

Eight

ANYBODY HAVING TROUBLES?

THIS is a short chapter—for those of you who got off to what you thought was a fine flying start and then ran into trouble. By trouble, I mean that you were going along happily, gracefully, forcefully, when suddenly your hero dropped dead, or the heroine turned into a shrew, or the villain turned to milk toast in his big scene. In other words, everything and everybody stopped moving and lay right down on the paper and died.

There may be one of several things wrong. A likely source of your trouble is that you don't want to write a particular story. Maybe it was the first story idea that occurred to you, and your first enthusiasm impelled you to try to write it. Maybe it's a story you will write some day, a story you should save for your old age, when, presumably, you will have the necessary wisdom and life experience to do it justice. Don't try to write something you are either not really interested in, or are unable to do justice to at this early stage of your writing career.

The cure for this trouble is simple. Try to find another story idea, one which appeals to you and one which you feel confident you can do successfully now.

Another possible source of trouble is that you are afflicted with a certain shyness about writing in general. You feel a great urge to write, an even greater urge to write the particular story you have settled on, but there is a reticence about jumping off into the actual writing. You feel, consciously or subconsciously, that you are exposing yourself in public, walking down Main Street without your clothes on. The only advice I can give you is that you'll just have to get over it. The thing to remember is that the truly skillful writer is invisible to his readers. The truly skillful writer can walk down Main Street again and again, naked as a jay bird, but his readers will never see him. They're too busy watching the other people he's showing to them.

The most likely cause of trouble is that you may not have set your story up right. This is especially true if you have trouble more than halfway through your story. If this is your trouble, acknowledge it. Get up and walk away for a while; don't just hunch there in front of the typewriter. That one thing accounts for more fatalities among stories than any other!

Walk away; go some place quiet and unpeopled; wash dishes; wash the car; bake a cake; mow the lawn; take a sun bath. Play cat with mouse. Lift your big, fat, determined paw off your poor, shivering, no longer challenging creature of a story idea. Let it go, turn your back, and more than likely it will come to life again.

When it does, seize it, devour it, taste it, digest it slowly and thoroughly. To your eternal surprise you may find that it wasn't a mouse at all. Instead, it was a gopher, a mole, a rabbit.

For instance, you may have thought you were writing about a noble, dutiful daughter who forgoes love and marriage to stay home and care for her aged mother. You may have set the story up as such, when, actually, the story you want to write, the story you are equipped to write, the story which burns in you is one of foolish martyrdom eventually giving way to the magnificent demanding starburst of a woman's love for a man.

In this case, go back and begin again and write the story you really wish to write—not the story you feel you should write.

Perhaps the commonest source of trouble midway through your story is that you are pouring all your energies and thought and craft and worry into perfecting the *plot,* to the detriment of your real story, which is the *people* in your story. The important thing in a story is the people and their emotions, the story which happens inside them. The characters should move about on the stage of life instead of being moved about like paper figures, willy-nilly and without motivation except what comes from you, a puppeteer determined that so-and-so shall go through a certain door at a certain time, because only by doing so, can so-and-so bump into so-and-so; so that two pages later so-and-so can say . . . and so on and so on and so on.

Stop worrying about the plot. Write the story. Make the reader laugh, make him cry—not by opening and closing doors on some mechanical timetable, but by fitting his hand in the hand of your hero so that he feels the doorknob under his hand as your hero turns it. Even though a reader may *know* what lies on the other side of the door, he can still open that door suspensefully, suffering and anticipating and dreading with your *unknowing* hero.

Never forget that your reader has a double pleasure: knowing all, or what he assumes to be all, with you, the writer; and, at the same time, knowing nothing, suspensefully, with your hero—going along for the ride to see how your hero will conduct himself when he must face his own specific moment of truth and do something about it.

Nine

AILING STORIES: DIAGNOSIS AND CURE

AT LAST, you have finished your story. At least, you think you have finished it. You have anywhere from five to twenty-five pages, and in your emptied, charred state, after burning so brightly for so long, you feel that surely with all this effort you have accomplished what you set out to accomplish—the writing of a story which some editor will think interesting enough to enough readers to be bought for money and transformed by the magic of slick magazine print and a slick magazine illustration.

Weak as you are, you want to read it quickly and make sure that you have what you think you have. Don't! Go outside; have a Coke, take a walk, or play a game of golf; in other words, *get away from it*. Work some of the carbon out of your head by working your unused muscles, and then when you absolutely can't stand it any longer, come back and read it.

Read it the first time, not as the author, but as a reader, at a reader's rather swift pace.

I was once asked by a student if it would perhaps be helpful to read the new story aloud or have it read aloud. Not on your life! Most stories today (and this is especially true of slick fiction stories) are not and should not be written to be read aloud. They are read silently by readers in a hurry. Reading your own story aloud or listening to it being read aloud is the equivalent of reading it word for word, and that is a very unfair and misleading test to apply at this time.

To see what I mean, why don't you take the latest issue of one of the slick magazines and sit down and read, either aloud or to yourself, word for word, one of the stories which you enjoyed very much. It's amazing how pedestrian and trite and labored even the best of writers come out when read in this way. Offhand, I can't think of anyone who could pass this test.

Give your story a chance. Read it the first time more or less as it would be read by the reader of a magazine story already in print. In this manner, you can more effectively judge the story as a whole, not just that beautiful phrase on page four or the smooth transition on page eight, but the whole story in terms of story accomplishment—tone, pace, the story itself—which lives or should live in the flesh and bones of your hero, not in the clothing you have provided him.

Now you have read your story straight through, without interruption, for the first time: *Is it a story? Are you finished with it?* You aren't, unless you are a genius, or it happens to be one of those lucky stories that fly by themselves.

This is the time to cease being creative, to cease burning brightly, to stop being proud of yourself just because you did this marvelous thing. It may not be a marvelous thing—it may be awful. You must recognize this, even if it kills you. Then you must do something about it. If you are incapable of doing something about it at this tender time, put the story away. Refrigerate it for a while. If you still have an ounce of energy left, save your refrigeration period for that time between the second draft and the final copy.

Whichever way, let's now pretend that the time has come to do something about it. But what? That depends on what the trouble is. I have made up a list of twelve story ailments and some things you can do about each of them.

1. THE STORY THAT WON'T BREATHE. No wonder it won't breathe; it has no life. You can't say it's dead, for it hasn't been around long enough to tell about that. It looks fine. Fifteen pages of double-spacing, and the title is wonderful, but it just lies there. The trouble with this story is that even though you have just performed the marvelous feat of creating it, more or less single-handed, and though it has the appearance of a living thing, perfectly formed, even handsome in all its details, it is not alive in the way that we know and term life. It doesn't breathe.

There's only one thing to do: Apply artificial respiration; breathe into it the living breath of life from yourself, *your* personal experience with life, *your* knowledge of hope, fear, love, hate, happiness. Breathe strongly, surely, until your story cries out with breath of its own, until it opens its eyes and looks back at you, the intermediary of its creation—out of living eyes as familiar and mysterious as the eyes of your own children. For new life has always some of the mysterious, something of the miraculous, even for the one who created it. When you have done this, then and then only will you know that you have written a good story.

2. THE WANDERER. This story ambles all over the place. You know why? Because when you started, you didn't know where you wanted to go. If you didn't know, your hero certainly couldn't be expected to know where he was going!

Your story always goes with your hero. If your hero is allowed to poke around in every alley he passes, to amble lazily down every tree-shaded lane, to drop in to visit Aunt Minnie on the way to his own personal moment of truth, your reader is going to get the idea, quite rightly, that your hero's moment of truth isn't so important after all. Cut out the excursions, the visit to Aunt Minnie, and go straight down the road.

3. THE FISHY STORY. The trouble with this story is that it ain't true. By true, I don't mean the content, which for some stories can be as wild as any fisherman's tall tale. What I mean is that you didn't believe it while you were telling it.

The biggest and best liars may know the instant before they open their mouths, and possibly the instant after they close their mouths, that what they are going to tell and what they have just told is not technically true. They do not believe their own story, but—and this is the important thing—*while they are telling their story, it is true and they believe it.*

This is an antic point of view, a perverted faith—call it what you will—which many storytellers possess and which enables them to tell any story believably, *because they believe it themselves during the telling.*

Don't attempt to tell stories you cannot believe, at least during the telling, or yours will be a Fishy Story. Any story comes out a Fishy Story, if the writer cannot believe it while he is writing it. If you, the writer, believe it, your readers will believe it; if you don't, they won't. Put aside the story you can't believe until that day in the future when you can believe it long enough to write it convincingly. Incidentally, the Fishy Story is usually burdened with too many bones, a too intricate and plotty plot. Realizing you do not believe, you attempt to convince yourself by an excess of mechanical maneuvers.

4. THE UNFINISHED SYMPHONY. This title speaks for itself. For one reason or another, you didn't write the whole story. Sometimes this happens because a writer is lazy or beset by interruptions, or hollow-stomached and unreasonable from hunger, and desirous of a quick check.

At some point in writing a story, the writer may have the illusion that the story is finished, when it really is only partly written—because as the writer he knows what is going to happen in the story before it is revealed and known to the reader.

All I can say about the Unfinished Symphony problem is that many highly skilled writers seem to get away with a remarkably small portion of their stories on paper. If you study these stories carefully, however, you will find that what is on paper, in print, is so powerful and provocative and telling in itself that even though the rest of the story "isn't there," you can see it.

No reader can help but see the whole story and understand the theme and purpose of it—so wondrously wrought is the part that *is* written. For writers less skillful, and that includes most of us, it is a dangerous practice to tell only part of the story in the hope that the reader will imagine the rest of it. Every story that the average author writes should have a beginning, a middle, and an end; each section is as important as the other. Most slick fiction editors rarely buy the "unfinished symphony" type of story. They prefer a good, *complete* story with an unbroken story line.

The cure for this kind of "unfinished" story is for the writer to get back in there and *finish the story*.

5. THE ZOMBIE. The ailment or weakness in this type of story is infinitely more serious than The Story That Won't Breathe. This story gets up and walks around, after a fashion, and talks, after a fashion, but, except in a ghoulish sense, it is not entertaining. It is certainly not heartwarming or moving or endearing or exhilarating, humorous or romantic. It is simply disagreeable.

This kind of story is written by many otherwise competent writers every once in a while. Each of us has at least one peculiarity which does not deserve to see the light of day. When, unknowingly, we create a story out of this peculiarity, we have written a Zombie.

If, in spite of fine writing and a well thought-out conclusion and story line, in spite of your story's walking and talking, you have an uneasy, unsatisfied, and faintly appalled feeling about a story, the chances are you have written a Zombie. You may even sell it— a few magazines publish one every now and then—but for heaven's sake, don't make a career of writing Zombies. They aren't nearly as much fun to write, in fact they're no fun at all, and the market for them is very small.

I know of no cure for Zombies. If you write one, there are two courses open to you: 1) get it in the mail and hope some editor is Zombie-minded at the moment it crosses his desk; 2) bury it with proper incantations, to make sure that the Zombie will never again arise.

6. THE OLD WISTERIA VINE. Again, the title speaks for itself. This is one of the commonest ailments a story can have. The nicest writers, especially beginning writers with the finest intentions in the world, turn these out. Zealous, dedicated, and outgoing, you write out your heart and soul, all of it—and then what do you have? Not one story, but two stories (or maybe even three!) irrevocably, or what seems irrevocably, entwined.

There they are, two or three separate stories, impossible to market separately, and unfeasible to try to market as one story, because with so many plots competing for attention, the distracted reader will be tossed about and will find it impossible to concentrate on anything. This is a bad situation, but not as bad as it first appears. Keep your head. Something must be done, and you are best equipped to do it because *you* raised this Old Wisteria Vine and let it twine itself into the unmarketable tangle it is now in! Make a thorough study of the situation. The task of disentangling the stories is by no means hopeless, but it can be done only if you keep a clear, level head.

Sometimes, if the stories share a common root (for instance, if both are dependent upon an unusual premise, the *same* unusual premise; or if they depend on the same striking, specific—not general—opening or closing situation), it may be necessary to sacrifice one story to the other or others. This is a last resort, however, and need be only temporary, for if you can bear to wait, the editors will be receptive, eventually, to *another* story about *another* man who solved his domestic crises by moving into a tree-house in his own back yard.

In most cases, the shared root can be replaced by grafting or a substitution in one of the stories, so that both may be saved and both marketed. But, whichever is the case, the disentangling must be done, painful as it may be. For whatever comfort it may give, let me remind you that two checks are usually, almost always, better than one!

Another bit of comfort I'd like to offer is that from personal experience I have found that the longer I write, the fewer Old Wisteria Vines I end up with. My last one was written several years ago with great care and fervor. Recognizing only that the story was somewhat over-long, I sent it to New York and it was submitted to *Good Housekeeping*, from which it came back with a lengthy comment showing that they cared for the story, and containing a number of suggestions for its revision. (This is almost invariably the maddening way with an Old Wisteria Vine story. Nobody buys, but everybody wants to get into the act and help out.)

In light of the comments, I studied the story and worked on it, still unaware of what I had done. When you have written as long as I have, you can entwine two

and even three stories pretty completely. The amount
of skill necessary to untwine them is in direct ratio to
the amount of skill which went into entwining them in
the first place!

At long, long last, it dawned on me that what I had
was the dramatized synopsis for a one-shot novel, complete even to sub-plots, wrapped around a very deli-
cate, tender, little story of a girl on the eve of her wedding.

I must confess I haven't found time to separate the
two stories, but I'll get around to it one of these days.
Lifting out the little wedding eve story will be a simple matter, in spite of its sharing a vital root with the
other story. I'll simply use the root for this short story,
and grow another in the meantime for the one-shot.
There'll be plenty of time for that before I find the
time to dig in and expand that synopsis into the one-
shot it should be.

7. The Tall Paul. This sad story has one thing in
common with the Old Wisteria Vine. It's far too long,
but there the similarity ends. Tall Paul isn't too long
because it contains several stories. There's nobody
home in this story except Paul, who goes on and on forever, stretched out and out interminably by his creator
in the hope that by length alone, Tall Paul would reach
the sky and stand with his head in the stars.

This is a story in which the good, interesting, even
powerful small story is made impossibly and boringly
thin by long narrative stretches which serve only as
transitions between the important scenes.

A reader doesn't have to be subjected to every curve
and bend in the hero's long, long road. Tall Paul has

the monotony, the interminable time element of real life itself—so many hours when absolutely nothing of importance happens.

People who write this kind of story need to realize that a clean break between scenes of importance is the more effective procedure. As Andy Griffith so ably put it in his folk version of the opera *Carmen*, summing up the events between one act and the next, "And time passes."

The movies used to make transitions by flipping the leaves on a calendar. There are always ways and means to prevent a Tall Paul story's uninteresting growth. Cut the transition narrative by a foot or so, and you'll discover a new story, effectively in proportion and most attractive.

8 THE LAZY LOUISE. This story isn't skinny—quite the contrary! It may have started life in its creator's mind as a lithe sylph, but after a steady diet of details ("hot biscuits light as feathers, rich as cream," "home-made strawberry jam with the aroma of heaven," "blueberry muffins as tender as young love," etc.), the original trim story line is lost. The story's fine bone structure is covered. Lady writers are often guilty of using this type of gastronomical detail, or of lovingly describing modernistic paintings, Victorian furniture, and all that goes to make up decor and furnishings—to the detriment of the story scenes which occur in the room described.

The cure for the Lazy Louise story is to put it on a diet. If tender, flaky biscuits are necessary to your story, leave in just one biscuit. Don't keep bringing out a fresh, hot panful from the kitchen. In the limited boundaries of a short story, one taste of homemade strawberry jam is worth an entire pantryful. The first biscuit with jam, your reader will eat with delight. Any more will make him heavy with boredom.

If you must describe room furnishings, the best way is to select one piece which has meaning in your hero's or heroine's life, which does something for the story, which means something to the story. Out of a whole living room of furniture, the only meaningful piece for a short story might be an old chair upholstered in beige leatherette ten years ago by the heroine when she and her husband were going to college and living on love. That chair means something; let the rest of the furniture go. Trim your over-detailed story down, and your reader will see it for the sylph it truly is.

9. THE HEARTBREAKER. This is a story which first gladdens and exalts your heart, then breaks it. It is just what the name implies, and there is no explaining or understanding or curing its defect. Editors will admire but continue to reject The Heartbreaker, no matter how cunningly you rework it or how carefully you choose your markets. I have written several such stories, and whether the fatal defect is in the material or in the way in which I used it; whether the trouble stems from the words I used to write the story or from the fact that I wrote and rewrote with such care and intensity (perhaps *too much* intensity, *too much* polishing and repolishing? This could be the case: it is said that we kill the thing we love . . .), I do not honestly know.

The Heartbreaker is like a happy dream that turns inexplicably into a nightmare. There is nothing to do with it but put it away. I cannot even discuss my Heartbreakers with humor. When and if you write a Heart-breaker, you will understand what I mean.

10. THE FRENZIED STORY. This story is good to begin with, but it ends up all over the place, constantly annoying the reader—supplicating, beseeching, ingratiating, to the point of frenzy.

The trouble with The Frenzied Story is that the writer was trying too hard. Many amateurs are guilty of this, and sometimes professionals after an unseemly number of rejections or setbacks. The Frenzied Story is very wearing both on you, the writer, and on your reader. Calm down, take it easy; stop imposing your own anxious desire to please on your hero or heroine.

The best way to please is to entertain, not to force your reader to sit forward apprehensively on the edge of his chair to witness a performance so patently a bid for favorable attention that it is downright tiresome. The reader's strongest desire is to avert his eyes from the spectacle.

As I said in the first chapter, it is best not to think of such personal things as need for money while actually writing your story. Maintain your personal dignity at all cost. If you have temporarily lost it, go back somewhere and find it. The Frenzied Story will then settle down and become the good, entertaining story it should have been in the first place.

11. THE SWAMI STORY. In this story, you made the mistake of revealing yourself to your reader, as you sat high up on your lonely, grand mountain top. What was worse, you leaned down and patted your reader on the head, patronizingly, from the solitary splendid height of your experience and wisdom. You

may actually be wiser than all your readers put together; you may be a genius and a noble humanitarian rolled into one—but never under any circumstances should you let your reader feel this.

You have a story to tell, and that's all you should do. Your story will, if you are skillful and truly wise, reveal your wisdom and compassion in a way so entertaining, so personally impersonal, that your reader will never think of resenting you. To accomplish such a thing, *you* must stay out of it. You can't pat your reader on the head—even if he happens to be a very young child —and say, patronizingly, "Now, now, my dear," and expect him truly to love and respect you. Yes, you *are* seeking love and respect, not for yourself personally, you protest, but for your stories. But aren't your stories as personal as your own flesh and blood?

Go through The Swami Story and keep yourself out of it. Whatever you do, don't pat your reader on the head—he won't like it.

12. THE CHEATER. This is the meanest problem story of them all. The Cheater doesn't *give*—it doesn't make that gift of love about which I spoke earlier; it simply tries to *get*. Recognition, money, fame, prestige, money. . . . This is the hollow story, the story without a heart, because you didn't put yours in it. This lack shows up because writing is the most personal of all the creative arts.

You, as an identity, may not be—and most probably are not—in your story at all, but you, the creator, spring up, nevertheless, with every word, like the force in the fountain which sends each droplet skyward. You *are* your story, and you show to advantage or to disadvantage—rather plainly and clearly.

In your writing you give yourself away in both senses of the phrase: You tattle on yourself and/or, ideally, give yourself. But what is life besides giving yourself? A bit here, a bit there. To give joyously, freely from the heart, is to gain the world.

Acting is also a very personal giving, but in acting you give yourself to the role, to *one* role, for you obviously cannot play more than one role at once. A writer plays *every* role in his story, including the setting in which his story is laid, the air his hero breathes. A writer is and should be all over the place, giving himself away totally. So don't put on a giving face when you are really not giving at all. It will show up in the Cheater Story. You will be as sounding brass and tinkling cymbal, like the little child running with his drawings to his mother, saying, "Look what I did, Mommy! Look what I did!" And when his mother, amazed, says, "Darling, did you draw that all by yourself?", he lifts up his little face and says "Yes!" Unfortunately, your reader doesn't have a mother's blind faith in your words or your ability; your reader knows darned well you traced the picture! Most Cheater Stories are imitative either in plot or style. Don't imitate; create for yourself. Don't just try to get; *give,* and, you'll never be guilty of writing The Cheater.

There are my twelve story ailments. You may think of others. Whatever your eventual list, learn to recognize these problem stories and do something about them—even if you do nothing more than recognize that nothing can be done. Sometimes that is the case, but don't be lazy and consign all ailing stories to the trash can. In most cases, something can be done to save them; if you don't try to save them, it's a terrible waste. Assuming that you are a sensible writer and are not going to indulge in waste, you will revise and revise and revise again, if necessary, aiming always for that absolutely superb *final* final copy.

Ten

THAT *FINAL* FINAL COPY

YOU'RE almost there! Almost ready to stand in the post office and watch that Manila envelope disappear down the Outgoing slot, that Manila envelope containing your heart, your hopes, and 15-17 pages of the best short story writing you are capable of.

But before you actually go "There," go over your story carefully once more. Go back to the original concept of the story; if all of the pieces do not seem to fit, revise accordingly. When you find that you must revise, don't do a patch job.

It may simply be that you have used the wrong viewpoint character. Usually your hero or heroine is the viewpoint character, but that isn't an unbreakable rule by any means. Sometimes your hero's story can be told most effectively from another character's viewpoint.

Sometimes, though rarely, you have placed your story in the wrong setting—in the city when it could best be told in the country. Or maybe you have overpowered a slender story with an unnecessarily exotic setting. Imagine your story in another setting, in several different settings. You may be surprised.

To illustrate how important setting can be in real life, think of the single piece of jewelry magnificently displayed on black velvet in the jeweler's window. How rich and enticing it looks, solitary and uncluttered, nesting on the stark softness of black velvet. In contrast, think of the small-town, cut-rate dry goods store, the windows overcrowded to the point where the lovely dress or hat is completely lost among children's socks, men's sport shirts, levis and work shoes, and swim suits for the entire family.

The easiest way to get editors to vie with each other to provide your surplus stories with good homes is to love and cherish the stories yourself, I have discovered; to display them like gems on the tender velvet of your own affection.

If you, the author, don't think enough of your own creation to display it in a setting which complements instead of detracts, which shows the story to best advantage—if you don't love your own story enough to display it with intelligent loving care, then no editor or reader is going to think it is worth very much. So change that setting if necessary.

Then there is the hero who cannot or will not stay in character to do the things you wish him to do, which he must do for the sake of the story. If such is the case, motivate him so he cannot help doing the proper thing when the time comes. If he cannot be so motivated, perhaps his character needs changing, perhaps his character is not at peace and harmony with the story. If his character can be changed, then change it. If not, create another hero who will do the thing he must do, who will do it naturally and inevitably and, to your reader, satisfyingly. But don't throw away the hero who didn't fit this particular story! Save him—he'll probably do for another story some day.

You must, of course, cut Tall Paul and Lazy Louise. If you must cut, be quick, incisive and decisive. After all, your story's life is at stake. *Be ruthless, but don't be deadly*. It's pretty hard to cut a good story to death, but it can be done, it has been done.

Most writers, however, aren't so ruthless, at least with their own stories; they're "chicken." Their impulse is to take the story to someone else, perhaps a friend who also writes, and ask him to point out where it can be cut. This is a mistake. No one can cut your story as well as you. Cutting at its finest is also creating. When you are creating, you stand alone.

Nobody can write your story but you. By the same token, nobody can cut it and reshape it better than you. You know its bones, its idiosyncrasies, its soft spots and hard spots, better than any other person on earth can be expected to know them. Do your own cutting with a quick and skillful hand. Watch particularly for the redundant phrase, the redundant paragraph, the redundant sequence of emotional or physical action, and especially, the redundant member of your cast. Very often in a drastic cutting job, one character can do the work of two.

If you'd like to study the way in which stories can be telescoped, you might dig out the old issues of *Redbook* and *Cosmopolitan* containing the stories I have used as illustrations in the preceding chapters, and compare the telescoped versions with the published versions.

When you are finally satisfied with your story, when you're exhausted and spent and you know you can do no better, there is yet one final chore. But let's not call it a chore! Let's think of it as those last little things a mother does before she sends her child off to the birthday party, to the recital, to school, to the first dance. That last loving bit of grooming.

Maybe there's a word on page four that doesn't sound quite right. Replace it with a better word. Maybe there's a fuzzy sentence on page six. Clarify it. Maybe there's an out-of-character bit of dialogue. Refashion it.

The first paragraph and the last can always use a bit more punch. Remember that the first paragraph must be provocative, as provocative as you can make it. The last paragraph must be as satisfying as you can make it.

When the final grooming is done, send the story off and forget it. You may as well. If you have an agent, you will come closer to forgetting it than if you are submitting direct. But direct submission can be enjoyable, too. Play a game with the editors. Your stories are your cards. Play them out wisely. Hit the same editors with good stories and keep hitting them at well-spaced intervals to show that you are capable of producing and continuing to produce good stories; to show that you aren't a Johnny-one-note, or a dilettante who will soon be bored with writing.

Don't cry over rejection slips. Don't take them too seriously. If an editor says a specific thing is wrong with your story, most likely there is *something* wrong, but in all probability it's something different from what the editor says it is. This is not intended as a slur against editors. Most of them are not working writers and all of them, I'll wager, are very busy. They haven't the time or the faculty, even when they like your story, to revise it for you. It's up to you to find out what needs changing and to change it.

When an editor suggests that you should do a specific thing here and a specific thing there and goes to the trouble to state exactly what he wants, that's another matter. You are on the brink of a sale and unless the specific changes violate every premise on which you founded your story and by which you live, immediately do exactly those things, to the best of your ability, which the editor has asked you to do. You may even sell the story—although this doesn't necessarily follow.

In the case of conflicting comments from different editors, neither of them very strong or very specific, either ignore both and keep sending the story out as it is, or revise according to the comment which seems most valid to you—but only if you yourself feel that the story needs revision. Remember that editors' comments are geared to the moment in which they are made—to the particular needs of the magazine at that moment, to the stories in inventory at that particular moment, to the stories scheduled for the next issue. The story needs of a magazine change from moment to moment, and no two magazines have exactly the same story needs at the identical time.

If your story, even in the face of several rejections, is still valid and satisfying to you, have faith in it. Don't mutilate it in accordance with some editor's momentary need or whim. It is only after specific direction from an editor who sincerely wishes to buy your story that you should make drastic changes. Or, if you have accumulated a sheaf of comments, all of which form a cohesive pattern of error on your part—if, for instance, more than two editors are unanimous in the opinion that your story starts too slowly—then you must seriously consider cutting the underbrush out of the beginning, sharpening it and bringing it into focus.

If, even after painstaking revision, a story does not sell, then bury it in your file. But don't bury yourself with it. You have many other stories to write. *Write them.*

And each time you sit down to the typewriter or tape recorder or clipboard, remember that you are not alone. Many others are writing, too. Remember, also, that even in the slightest story you are presenting people in a moment of truth. Remember that the most marketable truths are those which people most want to hear. If you must illustrate truths which people cannot bear to hear, don't write slick fiction short stories. Write novels. Until you are capable of writing novels, at least until you have written long enough to have gained considerable wisdom and skill, write those truths which people most want to hear and will most readily accept. Don't look upon or despise the common grass-root truths. They are time-strong and time-proven, most easily understood and accepted.

Don't bemoan the fact that your truth must be put into a capsule, that tight little, right little world of plot—fabricated, foreshortened, exaggerated, and, to be perfectly frank, usually trite and not even of itself true. Don't worry about the lie of plot. Remember that a writer is at once the biggest liar in the world and the most fervid, devoted teller of truth. That is your calling, and you're stuck with it. Make the most of it.

Know that you have a creative cycle, and take fullest advantage of it. Do your composing during those days of exultant creativity when you can almost literally do no wrong. And when the exultant days taper off, as they invariably do, into a more reasoning, cautious, thoughtful period, which too often is thought of as a "slump" but is actually the critic in you coming to the rescue, you'll have plenty of work for the critic—evaluation and revision, which are the critic's forte.

Use each different phase of your creative writing cycle for purposes best suited to it.

This comes under the heading of "reasonable inspiration." I have been asked if I wait for inspiration to write. If this question were put differently, "Do you write only when inspired?" I would answer an unqualified "Yes." As for the first question, "Do you wait for inspiration to write?" I would be forced to answer an unqualified "No." I write only when inspired, but *I don't wait for inspiration.* No writer can afford to, unless he is getting in the neighborhood of five hundred dollars a word.

As an adolescent, I waited for inspiration. Consequently, I can put almost everything written during that time into one Manila file. Don't wait for inspiration. Make your own. Any writer with any volume of output at all must generate his own inspiration. Believe that writing is a glamorous enterprise, a romantic enterprise, a heroic enterprise. By its very nature, it *is* all these things.

Let the excitement of your craft claim you. Excitement is stimulus; stimulus regenerates.

Please don't fall into the writers' common trap of thinking "nobody cares." For what it's worth, I care. I care so much about you and your writing talent and what you do with it that, in spite of the fact that I don't believe writing can be taught like algebra or dressmaking or bricklaying, I have presumed to try.

If I have confused or frightened you, I am sincerely sorry. If I have disappointed you by failing to give some magic cut-and-dried formula by which you can write a salable short story in your sleep or with half your brain and none of your emotion, I'm not sorry!

The best thing for any writer is not that he be handed a set of instructions for assembly like those which come with children's toys, but that he take joy in writing. The writer who takes joy in writing will instruct himself far better than I, or anyone else, can ever instruct him.

The greatest value that can come from taking a writing course is that it keeps you writing. It is primarily designed for that purpose. It was for that same purpose that this book was written—to *start* you writing, to *keep* you writing, and to *help* you understand that writing can be a very rewarding pleasure in itself.

It isn't everybody, remember, who can live simultaneously on both sides of the moon—the bright, benign front side and the dark, unknown back side. That's *you,* out there, I'm talking about. You are one of the few people in the world who can do the impossible. *You are a writer.*

THE END